D1612491

Together
with
Infants

Together with Infants

Themes and stories for assembly

Robert Fisher

Evans Brothers Limited

Published by Evans Brothers Limited
Montague House, Russell Square, London WC1B 5BX

Evans Brothers (Nigeria Publishers) Limited
PMB 5164, Jericho Road, Ibadan

First published 1982

Cover photograph by Jan Baldwin

Phototypeset by Tradespools Limited, Frome, Somerset
Printed and bound in Great Britain
by Spottiswoode Ballantyne Ltd, Colchester and London

ISBN 0 237 29352 8 NPR

Contents

Introduction   7

Themes   9

Stories   117

Prayers   173

Resources   187

    A Checklist of Resources   189

    Resource Books   190

How a theme can be related to all aspects of the curriculum

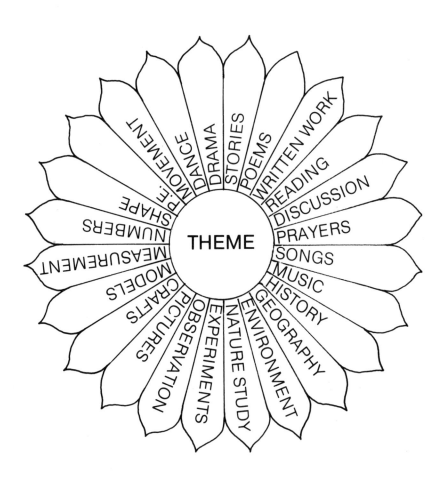

THEME

MOVEMENT
DANCE
DRAMA
STORIES
POEMS
WRITTEN WORK
READING
DISCUSSION
PRAYERS
SONGS
MUSIC
HISTORY
GEOGRAPHY
ENVIRONMENT
NATURE STUDY
EXPERIMENTS
OBSERVATION
PICTURES
CRAFTS
MODELS
MEASUREMENT
NUMBERS
SHAPE
P.E.

Introduction

All life is a meeting. *Together with Infants* is about making the most of meeting together with young children as a school, in a class or as a group. It is a book of resources which can be used in a variety of ways and adapted to suit individual requirements. Included are talking points, stories, poems, prayers, references to songs, and other suggested activities, all linked together as themes for assembly or classroom use.

Themes
The themes can be used for one assembly or for a series of meetings, and include ideas for preparation or follow-up work by children. The themes chosen aim to reflect the child's everyday experience, as well as extending that experience, together with information on major festivals, anniversaries and seasonal events. The assembly material is ideal for the planning of class assemblies, for group or solo presentation. Both teachers and children will be able to think of ways in which the material can be adapted or extended. The diagram on page 6 shows ways in which a theme can be related to a variety of creative activities.

Stories
The story section contains over fifty stories which may be read for their own sake by teacher or child, or used to illustrate a theme. Included are fables and folktales from Africa, China, India, the West Indies and other countries. These stories can be enriched by the use of mime, movement and drama. Presenters are encouraged to adapt and extend the stories as they think fit, for as Rudyard Kipling said:
'There are nine and sixty ways of constructing tribal lays,
And-every-single-one-of-them-is-right!'

Prayers
After the stories come a collection of prayers. These have been chosen to illustrate the themes, but these too may be found useful in other contexts.
A list of resources will be found at the end of the book.
Together with Infants is a companion to *Together Today* (Evans), themes and stories for assembly, many of which can be used with young children.

7

Themes

About me	12	Gardens	57
The Alphabet	13	Gifts	58
Autumn	14	Gold	59
Babies	15	Good Health	60
Bees	16	Halloween	61
Birds	17	Hands	62
Bread	18	Happiness	63
Calendar of Months:		Harvest Festival	64
January	19	Hobbies and Games	65
February	20	Holes	66
March	21	Homes	67
April	22	Hot and Cold	68
May	23	Ice and Snow	69
June	24	Journeys	70
July	25	Light	71
August/September	26	Listen!	72
October	27	Litter	73
November	28	Look	74
December	29	Machines	75
Canals	30	Mayday	76
Caring for Animals	31	Milk	77
Castles	32	Months of the Year	78
Caterpillars and Butterflies	33	Mothers	79
Chinese New Year	34	Numbers	80
Christmas	35	Our School	81
Christmas Customs	36	Pancake Day	82
Christmas Trees	38	People Who Help Us	83
Clothes	39	Pets	84
Colours	40	Pond Life	85
Communications	41	Protection	86
Creation	42	Proverbs and Sayings	87
Danger!	43	Rain	88
Dinosaurs	44	Remembering	89
Dragons	45	St Francis	90
Easter	46	Saying 'Thank You'	91
Easter Customs	47	The Sea	92
Eggs	49	Seeds	93
Fathers	50	Sheep	94
Favourite Things	51	Shopping	95
Feet	52	Signs and Symbols	96
Fireworks	53	Sleep	97
Flowers	54	Small Creatures	98
Forgiving	55	Spiders	99
Friends and Neighbours	56	Sports	100

Spring	101	Transport	109
Stars	102	Trees	110
Stones	103	Valentines	111
Strength	104	Who's Afraid?	112
Summer Holidays		Wind	113
At the Seaside	105	Winter	114
In the Country	106	Working Together	115
The Sun	107	World Family	116
Teeth	108		

Abbreviations

Song Books

CP	Come and Praise (BBC)
FFC	Faith Folk and Clarity (Galliard)
MHB	Morning Has Broken (Schofield and Sims)
NCS	New Child Songs (NCEC)
ONS	The Oxford Nursery Song Book (OUP)
Okki	Okki-tokki-unga (Black)
SSL	Someone's Singing Lord (Black)
TLP	This Little Puffin (Penguin/Puffin)

Poetry Books

B & P	Bits and Pieces (Black)
CFM	Come Follow Me (Evans)
FPB	A First Poetry Book (Oxford)
HL	Happy Landings (Evans)
J & J	Junket and Jumbles (Hamlyn/Beaver)
RAS	Round About Six (Warne)
S & D	Seeing and Doing (Thames TV)
SS	Skipping Susan (Evans)
WGMM	When a Goose Meets a Moose (Evans)
YP	The Young Puffin Book of Verse (Penguin)
YV	Young Verse (Armada Lion)

Story Books

TMAS	Tell Me Another Story (Puffin)
RMAS	Read Me Another Story (Hamlyn/Beaver)

Where full bibliographical information is not given for other books referred to in the Themes section this will be found on pages 190–191.

About Me

Theme   We are all different, no one is exactly like me. How are we different? We are all good at different things, we all have differing talents. We all look different, we sound different, and to animals we smell different! We are always finding out new things about ourselves, size of clothes, foods we like, etc. We need to take care of ourselves, and we must care for others too. Each one of us is important.

Stories   The Cat who kept her Name (p. 122)
The Parable of the Talents (*Matt.* 25)
Mr Men series   R. Hargreaves (Thurman)
The Book About Me   G. Wolde (Methuen)

Poems   Just Like Me   Anon. (HL p. 37)
You and Me (*Big Dipper* p. 4/5)
Sing a Song of People   Lois Leaski (YP p. 31)
My name is . . .   Pauline Clarke (YP p. 185)
A verse about Me   H. I. Rostron (*Poems for Movement* p. 120)

Songs   God Knows Me (CP no. 15)
If You're Happy (*Apusskidu* no. 1)

Prayers 27, 30, 35, 43, 48

Activities   Paint or draw self-portraits and portraits of friends. Print hand and foot shapes. Make pictures from fingerprints. Find out about your physical self—measure and record how tall and heavy you are, length of fingers, head-size, etc. Graph the colours of eyes and hair. Survey birthdays. Find out about skeletons, muscles, breathing rates, etc.

Note: See *All About Me* Schools Council Project on Health Education, Teachers Guide. 5–8 years (Nelson)

The Alphabet

Theme   There are twenty-six letters in our alphabet. These letters make up all the words that we speak, read or write. Like you, each letter has two names—the letter name, and the sound that the letter makes. Do you know the letter names from A to Z? There are two kinds of letters, big ones called capitals, and small ones. Capital letters are rather grand, they come at the beginning of names and of sentences. The first kind of writing used by people was made up of pictures. Later the pictures became letters. There are many kinds of alphabet in the world like Russian, Greek, Arabic and Hebrew. We use the Roman alphabet. From just twenty-six letters we can make every word in the English language. We can even make up new words. Can you think of a new word?

Story   *The Tragical Death of A, Apple pie, who was cut in pieces and eaten*
A was an Apple pie, B bit it, C cut it, D dealt it, E eat it, F fought for it, G got it, H halved it, I inspected it, J jumped for it, K kept it, L longed for it, M mourned it, N nodded at it, O opened it, P peeped at it, Q quartered it, R ran for it, S stole it, T took it, U upset it, V viewed it, W wanted it, XY and Z and ampersand all wished for a piece in hand.

Poems   A Nonsense Alphabet   E. Lear (*Rhyme Time* p. 21)
W   J. Reeves (J & J p. 14)
AEIOU   J. Swift (*Book of a Thousand Poems* p. 37)

Songs   The ink is black, the page is white (SSL no. 39)
A,B,C Tumble-down D (ONS p. 1)

Prayers 36, 57

Activities   Create your own illustrated alphabet books and friezes. Play letter matching, letter sorting, and word games, e.g. I-Spy. Make patterns using letter shapes, e.g. using letters cut from coloured sticky paper or drawing round templates. Show examples of alphabets from around the world. Collect different types of lettering from newspapers, magazines, etc. and make messages with them.

Autumn

Theme   Autumn is the season of harvests and of preparation for winter. In America it is called the Fall—what do you think falls in autumn? The autumn leaves often turn beautiful colours before they fall. Some animals go to sleep in autumn—they hibernate. Some birds fly away to warmer countries—they migrate. Farmers plough the fields and sow spring crops. At home we put on warmer clothes, and some families get fuel ready for winter to keep them warm. The days are getting shorter and each day it gets darker earlier. In autumn we put our clocks back one hour to make the most of the light in the mornings.

Stories   The Happy Prince p. 136
The Strange Treasure (*Together Today* p. 241)

Poems   Autumn Fires   R. L. Stevenson (HL p. 31)
Autumn Song   Ted Hughes (HL p. 33)
Autumn's Passing   H. I. Rostron (S&D p. 43)
Beech Leaves   J. Reeves (S&D p. 43)
Autumn Woods   J. S. Tippett (S&D p. 46)

Songs   Look for signs that summer's done (SSL no. 54)
The autumn leaves have fallen down (TLP p. 61)

Prayer   64

Activities   Paint a frieze showing autumn trees, falling leaves, seeds and fruits, animals and birds. Study leaf shapes, make leaf prints, leaf rubbings, leaf collages.
Movement themes—dance of the leaves, flight of birds, hibernation, farmers in the fields.
(See also Harvest Festival, p. 64)

Babies

Theme   We were all babies once. A baby needs food, warmth, clothes, washing and love. There are things he cannot do by himself such as walk, talk, eat, etc. The special things that babies need include a pram, cot, pushchair, feeding bottle, toys, nappies, etc. Most of all a baby needs love from his mother and other members of the family. At first all a baby seems to do is eat, sleep and cry. Babies are checked at the clinic, they are weighed and given injections. Babies are sometimes christened in church. What do you remember about being a baby?

Stories   Solomon and the Baby p. 165
The Monkey and her Baby p. 155
Jesus as a Baby (*Luke* 1&2)
The baby Moses (*Exodus* 1)

Poems   When I was One   A. A. Milne (*Now we are Six* Methuen)
Bringing up Babies   R. Fuller (RAS p. 32)

Songs   Bye Baby Bunting (ONS p. 26)
Hush-a-bye Baby (*Over and Over* p. 78)
John Brown's Baby (*Okki* no. 43)
Happy Birthday to You   Trad.

Prayers 19, 26, 27

Activities   Discuss how to look after a newborn baby. Visit a welfare clinic to see babies being weighed and measured. Ask a mother to show and talk about her baby. Display photos of the children as babies. Make a frieze or scrapbook showing the development of a baby brother or sister. Study and collect pictures of baby animals. Visit a zoo, pet shop or farm to see baby animals.

Bees

Theme   Have you ever heard of the saying 'busy as a bee'? What are bees so busy about? Bees fly from flower to flower collecting nectar and pollen. They carry it in special sacks in their legs back to their homes. Most bees live in hives, some live in wild nests. Beekeepers keep hives. They wear special clothes to protect them against bee stings. When a bee stings it dies. Each hive has a queen bee. She lays lots of eggs which grow into new bees. Bees make honey to eat. We like it too—honey is good for you! There is a lot to learn from bees.

Stories   Jupiter and the Bee p. 143
How the Bee Became   T. Hughes (in *How the Whale Became* Puffin)
Winnie the Pooh and Some Bees   A. A. Milne (Methuen)
The Queen Bee   Grimm (*My First Big Story Book* p. 92)

Poems   The Queen Bee   M. K. Robinson (CFM p. 18)
The Tale of a Dog and a Bee   Anon (CFM p. 209)
What do you suppose? (TLP p. 42)
Here is the Beehive (TLP p. 43)

A swarm of bees in May is worth a load of hay,
A swarm of bees in June is worth a silver spoon,
A swarm of bees in July is not worth a fly.

Songs   The Honeysuckle and the Bee (Music Hall Song)
The Beehive (*Sing a Song* 2: 114)
Music: *Flight of the Bumble Bee* (Rimsky-Korsakov)

Prayers 14, 61, 65

Activities   Make a mobile or collage of bees. Explore honeycomb (hexagonal) patterns, make equilateral triangles into hexagons, show how hexagons tessellate. Play games with hexagonal number spinners. Observe bees on flowers or visit an apiary with a glass-fronted observation hive. Make beeswax into candles or polish. Show how granulated honey can be made liquid again by standing jar in warm water. Invite a local beekeeper to talk about keeping bees.

Birds

Theme   In winter some birds fly off to warmer lands, others stay and need to be fed with bread and scraps. In the early spring birds begin to choose their mates and build their nests. Even in city streets you can hear the cooing of mating pigeons. Where do birds nest? Each type of bird builds a different kind of nest—most are pieces of straw and twigs woven together and lined with soft feathers. The different sorts of birds—sea birds, birds of prey, garden birds, farm birds, pet birds. Places where birds are kept—zoos, aviaries, cages, pigeon lofts. The beauty of birdsong, colour and flight. Conservation—the need to care for birds and not to steal birds' eggs.

Stories   The Happy Prince p. 136
Why the Robin has a Red Breast p. 169
St Valentine and the Birds (*Together Today* p. 230)

Poems   If I could have a pair of wings (YP p. 119)
Lollipops—section on Birds (Longman)
The Blackbird   Humbert Wolfe (*Bits & Pieces*)
Cheep!   E. Farjeon (TMAS p. 187)
Two little dicky-birds sitting on a wall (TLP p. 150)

Songs   The green grass grew around a little tiny bird (SSL no 24)
All things which live below the sky (SSL no. 41)
Little birds in winter time (SSL no. 43)
Feed the Birds (from *Mary Poppins*)

Prayers 2, 14, 53, 65

Activities   Try making a bird's nest out of straw, twigs, mud or clay. Make an origami bird beak from a square of paper. Visit an aviary or bird sanctuary. Collect and study feathers—investigate the saying 'as light as a feather'. Try writing with feather quills. Set up a bird table or nesting box. Keep a record book or graph of birds seen. Study bird movement—move like a bird.
    For further information contact: R.S.P.B.—The Lodge, Sandy, Berks, and The Wildfowl Trust—Slimbridge, Glos.

Bread

Theme   Bread is one of our most important foods. Eating bread gives us energy. Where does your bread come from—supermarket, bread shop, bread van or milkman? Bread really starts with wheat. The farmer harvests the wheat. The grain goes to the mill, where it is made into flour. The flour goes to a bakery to be made into bread. There are different kinds of flour and different kinds of bread. You can make bread yourself. How would you make it? There are many ways of eating bread, which is your favourite?

Stories   Five Loaves and two Fishes (*Matt.* 14)
The Little Red Hen   Trad. (Ladybird Books)
The Baker's Cat   Joan Aiken (*A Necklace of Raindrops*)
The Cargo of Wheat (*Together Today* p. 155)

Poems   Bread   H. E. Wilkinson (CFM p. 176)
The Baker   R. Talbot (SS p. 22)
The Mouse the Frog and the Little Red Hen (CFM p. 19)

Songs   When the Corn is Planted (SSL no 55)
Pat-a-cake, pat-a-cake, baker's man (ONS p. 29)

Prayers 40, 66

Activities   Count the seeds of grain on ears of wheat. Make a grain collage. Model with dough made from flour, salt and water. Make bread or bread rolls—work on measuring, weighing, shaping dough, baking time, effects of yeast. Graph or survey number of slices of bread the children eat in a day or week. Visit a mill or bakery.
     Movement theme—mills.

Simple Bread Recipe
Mix 1 teaspoon dried yeast and 1 teaspoon sugar in 150 ml warm water, leave in warm place for about 10 minutes till frothy. Mix 450 g wholemeal flour with yeast mixture and more warm water, add pinch of salt, and knead the dough. Put in greased tin, covered with damp cloth, in a warm place for about ½ hour to rise. Dust top with flour and bake loaf for 40 minutes (210°C, Gas mark 7).

Calendar of Months—January

January brings the snow
Makes our feet and fingers glow

January was named after the Roman god Janus who had two heads, one which looked into the past and one which looked into the future. Romans called him the keeper of the door who let the old year out and the new year in. (The word janitor meaning door-keeper comes from the name Janus).

Things to look out for Evergreens—holly, ivy and conifers, fallen cones and red berries (beware!). Watch for birds—robins, tits, blackbirds. Put out food for birds. Look for frost and ice patterns on windows or puddles.

1st January — New Year's Day. A holiday and time for celebration. Church bells are rung, and in Scotland there is a custom called 'first footing' when people visit their friends to wish them a Happy New Year. New Year resolutions are made and diaries for the year are begun. New Year's Day is the birthday of the year that has just begun. (See also: Babies p. 16)

6th January — Twelfth Night or Epiphany, because it is the twelfth night after Christmas and because the Christian festival of Epiphany celebrates the visit of the three Wise Men bearing gifts for the baby Jesus. It is the custom to take Christmas decorations down on Twelfth Night.

Plough Monday — The first Monday after Twelfth Night when ploughs were brought to Church for blessing, so that the farmer's crops would grow well.

25th January — St Paul's Day and Burns' Night. If St Paul's Day is fine it is said that harvest time will be good. Burns' Night is the time of grand dinners in Scotland to celebrate the poet Robert Burns who wrote the words of *Auld Lang Syne*. At this dinner haggis is eaten and bagpipes are played.

26th January — Australia Day, on this day in 1788 the first settlers arrived from Britain.

19

February

February brings the rain
Thaws the frozen ponds again

Named after the Roman festival of Februar. February is nicknamed 'Fill-dyke' because it is often a month of rain and melting snow.

Things to look out for   Flowering snowdrops and winter aconite, catkins on the trees. Leaf buds begin to show, yellow gorse is in bloom.

2nd February   Candlemas Day, also known as the feast of candles. It has its beginning in the old Roman festival of Februar when people carried lighted candles through the streets to celebrate the passing of the dark winter days. In Christian churches it is the feast of purification the date when the infant Jesus was presented in the Temple to be blessed. If you feel like celebrating too why not light a candle on Candlemas Day. (See also Light p. 71) An old weather rhyme says:

If Candlemas Day be fair and bright,
Winter will have another flight,
If Candlemas Day be cloud and rain,
Then winter will not come again.

14th February   St Valentine's Day (see also Valentines p. 111)
Shrove Tuesday (See Pancake Day p. 82)
Ash Wednesday The day after Shrove Tuesday and the first day of Lent.

Lent   Lent is an old Saxon word meaning spring. It was once the beginning of a long fast held in memory of the forty days Christ spent in the wilderness. Many people wore clothes made of sacking on this day, and were sprinkled with ashes by priests. This showed how sorry they were for the wrongs they had done. To help them remember people gave up something they liked during Lent.

Leap day 29th February   When Julius Caesar rearranged the calendar 2000 years ago every fourth year had an extra day in it, so whenever a year can be divided by four (e.g. 1984) February has twenty-nine days instead of twenty-eight.

March

March brings breezes loud and shrill
Stirs the dancing daffodil

March is named after Mars the Roman god of war. There is an old saying 'March comes in like a lion, but goes out like a lamb', because this month often begins with blustery windy weather and ends with mild gentle days. (See also Wind p. 113)

Things to look out for   Spring flowers—primroses, violets, narcissus, forsythia. Buds on the trees and the growth of bulbs. Birds begin nesting, migrant birds return. Hedgehogs and pet tortoises wake from hibernation. Look for frog spawn and pond snails. The birth of young animals on farms. Also mad March hares! (See also Spring p. 101, Pond Life p. 85, Sheep p. 94)

1st March	St David's Day, the patron saint of Wales, and his emblem is the leek. There are many old legends told about him and how the leek became his emblem. Daffodils are also often worn on this day by Welsh people. (See 'St David and the Leeks' *Together Today* p. 227)
17th March	St Patrick's Day, the patron saint of Ireland, many Irish people wear his emblem the shamrock. Many legends surround him. (See St Patrick *Together Today* p. 229)
25th March	The anniversary of the Angel Gabriel's visit to the Virgin Mary telling her she would be the mother of Jesus. In olden days children used to play a follow-the-leader game called 'Follow my Gable Ory Man' or 'Bangalory Man', meaning follow the Angel Gabriel.

Follow my gabelory man, follow my gabelory man
I'll do all that ever I can, to follow my gabelory man.
We'll borrow a horse and steal a gig,
And around the world we'll have a jig,
And I'll do all that ever I can, to follow my gabelory man.'

Mothering Sunday   Falls on the fourth Sunday in Lent, usually at the end of March. There are Mothering Sunday services in our churches, and children are often given small posies of flowers during the service to take home to their mothers.

April

April brings the primrose sweet
Scatters daisies at our feet

The name April is taken from the Latin word *aperire* which means to open out, because it is the time for the opening out of spring. April is famous for its showers. (See also Rain p. 88)

Things to look out for Wild spring flowers—dandelions, buttercups, daisies, violets, celandines. Blooms on the magnolia, flowering cherry and other blossom trees. Tulips begin to flower. The cuckoo is first heard in April.

The cuckoo comes in April, sings a song in May
In the middle of June another tune, and then he flies away

The sowing of seeds in gardens and allotments. (See also Gardens p. 57, Seeds p. 93)

1st April   All Fool's Day

The first of April some do say
Is set apart for All Fools Day
But why the people call it so,
Not I, nor they themselves do know
(from Poor Robin's Almanac 1760) April Fool's Day
is a day for playing tricks on everybody, from dawn
till midday. The ancient Romans knew the custom as
the Feast of Fools. French children call it *Poisson
d'Avril* or April Fish. It is said that in the old days
jesters were given a holiday till midday on 1st April,
so other people in the royal households had to play
the jester, hence All Fool's Day. (See *Together Today*
p. 16 for stories)

2nd April   Birthday of Hans Christian Andersen (1805) Danish
                   writer of fairy stories.
21st April   Birthday of H. M. Queen Elizabeth (born 1926)
23rd April   St George's Day, the patron saint of England, his
                   special flag is a red cross on a white background. (See
                   also Dragons p. 45)
25th April   St Mark's Day

Easter   often occurs in April. (See also Easter p. 46, Eggs p. 49)

May

May brings flocks of pretty lambs
Skipping by their fleecy dams

May is named after Maia, the goddess of Spring. More sunshine, but some days still cold, check the thermometer.

Here we come gathering nuts in May
Nuts in May, nuts in May
Here we come gathering nuts in May
On a cold and frosty morning

From this old song you can tell that May can be a cold month. So remember the old advice 'N'er cast a clout till May be out' (May is thought to mean hawthorn blossom) and 'Said the wise man to his son, 'keep on thy coat till May is done'.

Things to look out for   Hawthorn blossom, bluebells, wallflowers, tulips, lilac and horse chestnut. See which of these has perfume.

March winds and April showers,
Bring forth, May flowers.

You should be able to see caterpillars and butterflies by now, there are many insects, try looking at them with a magnifying glass. Birds are still nesting. Tadpoles developing back legs.

7th May	World Red Cross Day
12th May	Florence Nightingale born 1820
17th May	Edward Jenner, discoverer of smallpox vaccination, born 1749. (See also Good Health p. 60)
29th May	Oak Apple Day, celebrates the day in 1651 when Charles Stuart, son of Charles I, hid in an oak tree to escape the soldiers of Cromwell's army who were hunting him. Nine years later he returned to London as King Charles II on this same day, which was also his birthday.

Whitsun   Comes seven weeks after Easter, and often falls in May. Whit Sunday celebrates the coming of the Holy Spirit to the disciples (*Acts* 2)

Christian Aid Week   Usually comes in May.

23

June

June brings tulips, lilies, roses
Fills the childrens hands with posies

June is named after Juno, chief goddess of the Romans and Jupiter's wife. Summer has already arrived and it can be very hot (check the thermometer), this month is sometimes called 'flaming June' because of the heat, or perhaps because the roses are a blaze of colour at this time.

Things to look out for   Many wild flowers in woods and fields, the trees are in full leaf and there are many caterpillars. (See also Caterpillars p. 33) Smell the scents of flowers like honeysuckle and roses (especially on warm evenings). Shops are full of summer fruits, cherries, peaches, strawberries, etc. The days are long and the nights short—it is the opposite month to December. (See also Sun p. 107)

2nd June	Coronation of the Queen in 1953
10th June	Birthday of Prince Philip (born 1921)
15th June	World Children's Day (see World Family p. 116)
Fathers Day	occurs around 20th June (see Fathers p. 50)
21st June	The Longest Day—the summer solstice, after which the days start to get shorter again.
23rd June	Midsummer Eve
24th June	Midsummer Day—traditionally the time when Little Folk, or dancing fairies can be seen. (Hence Shakespeare's *Midsummer Night's Dream*). In the old days bonfires were lit to keep away fairies and evil spirits. At Stonehenge on Salisbury Plain people gather to watch the sun rise, and Druids hold ceremonies in honour of the sun. The great circle of stones at Stonehenge was built for the festival of the sun.
29th June	St Peter's Day

July

Hot July brings cooling showers
Strawberries and gilly-flowers

The month of July is named after Julius Caesar. July is often the hottest month of the year, but it is also a stormy month (see St Swithin below)

Things to look out for   Many insects—dragonflies, bees and wasps. Summer flowers and summer fruits.

4th July   Independence Day holiday in the USA. Americans celebrate this anniversary with parades and fireworks.

15th July   St Swithin's Day. An old legend says that if it rains on St Swithin's Day we shall have rain for forty days. Bishop Swithin lived in Winchester around the year 1100 and there are many stories of the wonderful things he did to help people, here is one of them.

One day an old lady was taking some fresh eggs to market to sell. As she was crossing a bridge she was jostled by a crowd of farmers leading their animals to market and she dropped and broke her eggs. Swithin saw what happened and bent to pick up her eggs and as he did so the old lady saw to her joy that they were whole again. Swithin was a humble man who wanted to be buried in a simple grave like ordinary folk, so when he died the people of Winchester buried him as he had wished, but later when he was made into a saint it was decided to move his grave into the cathedral. It was 15th July and it rained so hard that he could not be moved, and it continued to rain until they decided to leave the saint where he was, then it stopped raining. In all it had rained for forty days.

25th July   St Christopher's Day. (See also Journeys p. 70)

Swan Upping   A very old custom that takes place at the end of July every year on the river Thames. Swans have always been regarded as royal birds and the custom of marking the cygnets dates back to Elizabeth I.

Sports Day   (See Sports p. 100)

End of Term   (See Summer Holidays p. 105–6)

August/September

August bring the sheaves of corn
Then the harvest home is borne.
Warm September brings the fruit
Sportsmen then begin to shoot.

September was the seventh month in the Roman calendar, *septem* means seven in Latin.

Things to look out for   Signs of autumn, the flowering of dahlias and chrysanthemums, the fall of acorns and pine cones. Harvest fruits in the shops, apples, blackberries, figs, pears, plums. (See also Harvest Festival p. 64) The Autumn Term. (See Autumn p. 15) The New School Year. (See About Me p. 12, Our School p. 81)

21st September   St Matthew's Day
29th September   Feast of St Michael or Michaelmas Day
30th September   Feast of St Jerome (See Caring for Animals p. 31)

Jewish New Year (in September)   Rosh Hashanah the Jewish New Year Festival is also the celebration of God as the creator of the world and all mankind. Honey cakes or apples dipped in honey are eaten—honey is the symbol of hope and sweetness for the coming year. In the synagogue a ram's horn is blown during the New Year services.

Yom Kippur   The most holy day of the Jewish New Year, when Jews remember that God forgives those who are sorry for what they have done wrong. (See also Forgiving p. 55, also Jewish Festivals *Together Today* p. 67)

Muslim New Year   Called the festival of Muharram. The Muslim calendar is 354–355 days long i.e. ten or eleven days shorter than the solar year. New Year greetings are exchanged and stories of Muhammed told. (See Muslim Festivals *Together Today* p. 65)

October

Fresh October brings the pheasant
Then to gather nuts is pleasant

October was the eighth month in the Roman calendar, from the Latin *octo* meaning eight.

Things to look out for   Mushrooms and fungi growing from under fallen leaves, squirrels busy collecting nuts, birds feeding on the ripening berries, conkers (horse chestnuts), dying bracken, Michaelmas daisies, autumn crocus. Autumn fruits in the shops, flocks of birds migrating, falling seeds and spiders webs. (See Spiders p. 99, Seeds p. 93)

4th October	Feast of St Francis. (See St Francis p. 90)
12th October	Christopher Columbus Day (USA) America was discovered 1492. (See *Together Today* p. 156)
14th October	Battle of Hastings 1066
18th October	St Luke's Day
21st October	Trafalgar Day, Battle of Trafalgar 1805
24th October	United Nations Day. (See World Family p. 116)
31st October	Halloween. (See Halloween p. 61)

Divali (Diwali)   The Hindu and Sikh festival of lights falls in October or November. The word Divali comes from Diva meaning a lamp. The story of the festival is about the good king Rama who married the beautiful Sita. Sita was stolen by Ravanna, the demon king, and carried off. King Rama set off in pursuit, and with the help of the monkey army rescued the queen and returned to India in triumph. The festival celebrates the triumph of good over evil. To prepare for this festival homes are cleaned and lit with tiny lamps. Some Hindus make a large model of the demon king and burn it on a bonfire like our Guy Fawkes. Fireworks and crackers are let off to frighten away evil spirits. There are parties for children, presents are given and all share cakes and sweets. (See The Story of Divali *Together Today* p. 163)

November

Dull November brings the blast
Then the leaves are falling fast

November was the ninth month in the Roman calendar, *novem* means nine in Latin.

Ice in November, enough to hold a duck
All the rest of the winter will be mud and muck.
Note: In Australia this is the beginning of summer.

Things to look for   Fallen leaves making leaf mould for the soil. Fungus, lichens and moss. Fairy rings of toadstools, and ripening berries. Frosts and mists.

1st November	All Saints' Day—This is the feast day of all those saints who have no special day of their own. Also called All Hallows.
2nd November	All Souls' Day, for remembering ordinary people who have died.
5th November	Guy Fawkes' Day. (See also Fireworks p. 53)
11th November	St Martin's Day—Remembrance Sunday is the nearest Sunday to 11 November. (See also Remembering p. 89)
14th November	Prince Charles' Birthday (born 1948). A day to fly the Union Flag.
22nd November	St Cecilia's Day—the patron saint of musicians.
23rd November	St Clement's Day—Remember the bells? St Clement was drowned by being tied to an anchor, so he became patron saint of blacksmiths and iron-workers.
25th November	St Catherine's Day
Thanksgiving Day	Last Thursday in the month. (See Saying Thank You p. 91)
30th November	St Andrew's Day—St Andrew is the patron saint of Scotland. He was a fisherman who became a disciple of Jesus. The flag of Scotland is a cross because Andrew was crucified on an X-shaped cross. (See The Story of St Andrew *Together Today* p. 92)

The Lord Mayor's Show   On the second Saturday in November each year the newly-elected Lord Mayor of London leads a procession through the City to Mansion House to meet the Queen. The Lord Mayor travels in a special horse-drawn coach, and there is a parade of decorated floats.

December

Chill December brings the sleet
Blazing fire and Christmas treat
Sara Coleridge

This month was number ten, *decem* in Latin, before Julius Caesar changed the calendar.

Things to look out for   Christmas rose, holly berries, mistletoe, ivy and laurel leaves. Fruits in the shops now—melons, oranges, tangerines, nuts and dates. Christmas trees for sale. Birds you might see—robin, wren, peewit (lapwing), heron and ducks. (See also Ice and Snow p. 69, Christmas Trees p. 38)

Advent   Advent is the name given to the period leading up to Christmas, when we get ready for the coming of the baby Jesus. Advent calendars usually cover the twenty-five days from 1st December to Christmas Day, which is the birthday of Jesus. For each day of the calendar there is a picture to remind us of the coming event. Make your own advent calendar with surprise pictures.

6th December	St Nicholas' Day, the first Father Christmas, also called Santa Claus. (See Gifts p. 58)
13th December	St Lucia's Day, celebrated in Sweden. In the early morning a Lucia Queen, often the youngest daughter, dressed in white and wearing a crown of candles, visits each member of the family, bringing coffee and Lucia rolls.
21st December	Winter solstice/St Thomas' Day—the shortest day, only eight hours of daylight
24th December	Christmas Eve
25th December	Christmas Day (see Christmas p. 35)
26th December	Boxing Day/St Stephen's Day
31st December	New Year's Eve

Hannukah (Chanukah)   The Jewish festival of light which lasts eight days during December. It is celebrated by all Jews in the home and at the synagogue. Candles are lit in a special candlestick with eight holders, one on each day of the festival in memory of the re-dedication of the Temple of Jerusalem (see *Maccabees* 2.10) It is a time of gifts and parties for children. (See also Light p. 71)

Canals

Theme   Canals are waterways made by men. They were once a very important means of transporting goods. Canals have to travel on the level, so how could the water be made to go uphill? One of the tricks the canal makers used was the lock. A lock is like a lift which moves boats up and down. Tunnels and bridges (aqueducts) are among the ways of keeping the canal level when the land is not flat. For many years boats were towed by horses. People who worked the canals often lived aboard their boats. Old canal boats were often gaily painted and decorated. People used to live on these narrow boats—would you like to?

Stories   The Four Fools p. 131

Poems   Ten Little Narrow boats   T. Stanier (*Watch* p. 13)
The Growing River   R. Bennett (*Book of a Thousand Poems* p. 445)
The Old Man in a Barge   E. Lear (S&D p. 65)
The Tide in the River   E. Farjeon (S&D p. 65)
Where go the boats   R. L. Stevenson (*A Child's Garden* p. 32)

Songs   Rosie's Song (*Watch* p. 10)
Row, row, row, your boat (TLP p. 116)
One more river (ONS p. 72)
The ferryman (*Sing a Song* 2: 96)

Prayers 31, 53

Activities   Draw and decorate a picture or model of a canal boat. Measure out a canal boat cabin (3 metres long and 2 metres wide) and imagine living inside it. Find and study pictures of the canals in Venice. Visit a local canal or river, observe, draw and write about what you see. Look at a lock and see how it works. Find out about the Suez Canal and the Panama Canal.

Caring for Animals

Theme   We need to care for all animals—even wild animals. We care for wild birds in winter by feeding them. Some wild animals would die out altogether if we did not look after them and some organisations collect money to help care for wild animals e.g. RSPCA and the World Wildlife Fund. They do this by stopping animals from being hunted (e.g. elephants for ivory) and they give them places to live such as safari parks, game reserves, zoos. Many animals help man—farm animals, beasts of burden, police dogs and horses, circus animals. We need to care for our pets and all living things. There are many stories of saints and animals (see also St Francis p. 90)

Stories   St Jerome and the Lion p. 161
St Francis and the Wolf p. 160
Peter and the Wolf   Trad.
The Lost Sheep p. 147 (*Luke* 15.4)
Noah's Ark (*Genesis* 6)

Poems   Hurt no living thing;
Ladybird nor butterfly,
Nor moth with dusty wing,
Nor cricket chirping cheerily,
Nor grasshopper so light of leap,
Nor dancing gnat, nor beetle fat,
Nor harmless worms that creep.
                    Christina Rossetti

Kindness to Animals (CFM p. 157)

Songs   Who built the Ark? (SSL no. 44)
All things which live below the sky (SSL no. 41)
The animals went in two by two (*Apusskidu* no. 38)
Going to the zoo (*Apusskidu* no. 39)

Prayers 13, 15, 54, 65

Activities   Make a survey of pets. Show where endangered species live on a world map. Invite a speaker from the RSPCA or World Wildlife Fund. Listen to a tape of animal noises—can you identify each animal?
    Movement theme—be an animal to music such as *Carnival of the Animals* Saint Saens.

Castles

Theme   Have you ever built a sandcastle? Real castles can be very interesting places to visit. Castles are usually hundreds of years old. Many castles have fallen down and become ruins. Castles were built to keep enemies out. Some castles had moats of water all round them, with a drawbridge which could be pulled up and a portcullis to protect the door. Castles often have towers with narrow windows for shooting arrows through. The top of the castle walls were battlements behind which soldiers could hide. Underneath the castle were prisons called dungeons. The Tower of London is one famous castle. Do you know any others?

Stories   King Arthur and his Knights of the Round Table
Adventures of Robin Hood (Ladybird)
Meg's Castle   H. Nichol & J. Pienkowski (Heinemann)
Harum Scarum   Jany Barry (RMAS p. 58)

Poems   The Song of Alan-a-Dale   T. Stanier (*Watch* p. 45)
A Knight and a Lady   Anon. (YP p. 137)
Castles in the Sand   D. Baker (CFM p. 121)
Knight in Armour   A. A. Milne (*Now we are Six* Methuen)
Here comes a Knight   R. Fyleman (*Rhyme Time* p. 88)

Songs   When a Knight won his spurs (SSL no 34)
There was a princess long ago (*Okki* no. 20)
Will you come to my castle (*Sing a Song* 2 no. 63)
Robin Hood Song (*Watch* p. 42)

Prayer   6

Activities   Make a model castle out of boxes and card. Design your own flag. Make a life-size knight by drawing round a child, and cover with foil or milk bottle tops. Visit a castle or old church. Investigate the castle in chess, and other chess pieces. Refer to *Knights and Castles* Macdonald First Library, *Castles* Macdonald Starters Long Ago.
Movement theme—attacking and defending a castle.

Caterpillars and Butterflies

Theme   Butterflies are beautiful insects that come in many colours, shapes and sizes. Moths are like butterflies except they have thicker bodies and fly by night. Moths and butterflies feed mainly on nectar from flowers. Moths fly towards lights, and sometimes make holes in clothes. Butterflies and moths undergo a complete metamorphosis, or change, from egg, caterpillar, cocoon into adult. Many caterpillars weave a cocoon out of silk. Look for hairy caterpillars in spring—but be careful, they can give you a rash if you touch them. How a greedy caterpillar turns into a beautiful butterfly is something of a miracle, try seeing it happen.

Stories   The First Silkworms p. 127
The Very Hungry Caterpillar   E. Carle (Hamish Hamilton)
Two Green Caterpillars   M. Cockett (TMAS p. 192)

Poems   Brown and furry
Caterpillar in a hurry,
Take your walk
To the shady leaf or stalk.

May no toad spy you,
May the little birds pass by you.
Spin and die,
To live again a butterfly.
                    Christina Rossetti

The Tickle Rhyme   I. Seraillier (*Fancy Free* p. 18)

Songs   I went to the caterpillars (*Watch* p. 30)
Caterpillars only crawl (*Harlequin* no 26)

Prayers 13, 14, 54

Activities   Draw or paint the life cycle of a caterpillar. Collect and keep your own caterpillars, keep a caterpillar diary, measure the insect and see how much leaf he eats. Visit a butterfly or silk farm. Make a giant caterpillar e.g. with six children under two painted sheets and a mask. Make a butterfly mobile. Collect and study samples of silk.
    Movement—hatching chrysalis and butterfly dance.

Chinese New Year

Theme   Chinese New Year falls in January or February. It is a family festival which lasts for several days. It is a time when new clothes are worn, of visits to the family and friends. Gifts are exchanged. It is a time of new beginnings when debts are settled and houses cleaned. In areas where many Chinese people live, such as Soho in London, there is a great celebration with lion dances, coloured lanterns, peach blossom and firecrackers (used to ward off evil spirits). The Chinese say to each other 'Kung hei fat choy' which means 'Be happy and prosperous'. Lucky messages are written on red paper, and lucky money given in red envelopes.

Each year is dedicated to one of twelve animals. According to legend Buddha invited all the animals to come to see him, but only twelve turned up. So he rewarded the faithful by giving each one a whole year in turn. The Chinese believe that people inherit the characteristics of the animal in whose year they were born. Are you like the animal in your birth sign?

To find out the animal for each year, here is the 12 year cycle:

1972, 1984—Rat (or mouse)   1978, 1990—Horse
1973, 1985—Bull   1979, 1991—Goat (or sheep)
1974, 1986—Tiger   1980, 1992—Monkey
1975, 1987—Rabbit (or hare)   1981, 1993—Cockerel
1976, 1988—Dragon   1982, 1994—Dog
1977, 1989—Snake   1983, 1995—Pig (or boar)

Stories   The First Snow p. 128 or any Chinese folktale

Poem   Chinese New Year   D. Rickards (*Big Dipper* p. 106)

Song   Chinatown Dragon (*Harlequin* no. 24)

Prayers 19, 26, 44

Activities   Paint the animal associated with this year. Make a dragon for a Chinese dragon dance.
(See also Dragons, p.45)

34

Christmas

Theme   Every year in December we celebrate the birthday of Jesus Christ. Christmas really means the mass or the festival of Christ. We do not know the *actual* day Jesus was born on, but 25th December is the day when Christians all over the world celebrate his birthday.

At Christmas we remember that Jesus Christ taught us to love one another. We send cards and give presents to friends and relatives, and think of those people who are less fortunate than ourselves. We watch and take part in Nativity plays (Nativity means birth), and sing carols. We decorate our homes, schools and churches with fir trees, decorations, candles and coloured lights. We eat and drink good things, and have a happy time. We have Christmas parties to celebrate the birthday of Jesus.

There is another word that people use instead of Christmas, if they are lazy, and that is Xmas. The X stands for the Greek letter which is the first letter of Christ's name.

The Christmas story

An Angel visits Mary (*Luke* I)
The Journey to Bethlehem (*Luke* 2.1)
The Shepherds in the Fields (*Luke* 2.8)
The Coming of the Wise Men (*Matt.* 2.1)
The Flight into Egypt (*Matt.* 2)

Songs   Some collections of carols to discuss and sing:
Carol Gaily Carol   B. Harrop (Black)
Merrily to Bethlehem   D. Gadsby (Black)
Faith, Folk and Nativity   P. Smith (Galliard)
The Penguin Book of Christmas Carols   M. Poston (Penguin)
The Oxford Book of Carols (OUP)

Prayers 17, 42, 58, 59, 63

Christmas Customs

Theme   Where did our Christmas customs come from?

Holly   It is a holy tree that reminds us of the death of Christ. The prickly leaves are like the crown of thorns Jesus was forced to wear, and the red berries are like his drops of blood. In Norway and Sweden, holly is called Christ-thorn. Look out for holly wreaths.

Mistletoe   is an emblem of love, and so we have the custom of kissing under the mistletoe. It was sacred to the Druids and is never used to decorate churches. See the legend of Balder.

Lights   In many religions light is used as a symbol for truth. There are always candles on the altar of a church. Martin Luther first put candles on a Christmas tree to remind people of the stars that shone over Bethlehem when Jesus was born.

Carols   These were originally dances, holding hands, sung in memory of the birth of Jesus.

Cribs   St Francis is credited with making the first cribs. He wanted to show people what the stable was like where Jesus was born, so he arranged to have a live scene with real people, and a real ox and ass.

Christmas cards and crackers   date from Victorian times. The first crackers were called Bangs of Expectation with mottoes and charms wrapped in sweet paper.

Christmas pudding   was originally a plum porridge in which all sorts of things were put. Lighting of brandy dates back to the time of sun and fire worship.

Christmas presents   remind us of the gifts of the Wise Men and of God's great gift to us—his only son Jesus Christ.

Stories   Baboushka p. 120
Good King Wenceslas p. 134
A Christmas Legend   E. Colwell (*More Stories to Tell* p. 141)
see also:
Stories of our Christmas Customs (Ladybird)

Poems   Let's dance and sing and make good cheer
For Christmas comes but once a year.

Christmas Poems (*Book of a Thousand Poems* p. 530–548)
Christmas Poems (*Come Follow Me* p. 224–231)
A Single Star   anthology ed. D. Davis (Puffin)
Good King Wenceslas   Anon (*Round About Six* p. 55)
Advice to a Child   E. Farjeon (*Tell Me a Story* p. 173)
The Night before Christmas   C. C. Moore (RMAS p. 14)
Mincemeat   E. Gould (CFM p. 53)
Come Christmas   (*Rhyme Time* p. 173–183)

Christmas is coming, the geese are getting fat,
Please to put a penny in the old man's hat,
If you haven't got a penny a ha'penny will do
If you haven't got a ha'penny, God bless you.

Activities   Prepare a Nativity play, learn and sing carols. Create a
Christmas picture e.g. using silhouette cut-outs. Make a Nativity scene out
of modelling materials. Make and post Christmas cards in your own pillar
box. Display Christmas stamps, and design your own. Construct a Father
Christmas wishing box for children to write and put their wishes for
Christmas into. Make Christmas cake decorations, decorate a Yule Log.
Find out what 'Merry Christmas' is in different languages. Cut out and
decorate Christmas stars. Make Christmas crackers. Act out a traditional
pantomime story. Visit a local old-folks home to sing carols or bring
greetings. Refer to *The Christmas Book* S. Baker (Macdonald)
   Movement themes—a dance of the angels; following the star.

Christmas Trees

Theme   One of the loveliest of Christmas customs is the Christmas tree. A fir tree is brought into the house and decorated with tinsel, coloured lights and presents. This old custom was made popular by Prince Albert, the husband of Queen Victoria, who set up a tree in Windsor Castle in 1841. At Christmas time today there are hundreds of fir trees for sale, and one enormous tree is set up in Trafalgar Square, which is a gift from the people of Norway. There is an old tradition that the wood of the stable where Jesus was born was made from a fir tree. Many Christmas trees today are artificial. What are the differences between a real tree and an artificial one?

Stories   The Fir Tree p. 125
The Good Little Christmas Tree   U. M. Williams (TMAS p. 206)
The Surprise Christmas Tree   U. Hourihane (*Tell me a Story* p. 83)
The First Christmas Tree (*Together Today* p. 171)

Poems   The Christmas Tree   Anon. (*More Stories to Tell* p. 145)
Proud Little Spruce Fir   J. Kirby (CFM p. 99)
Little Tree   e. e. cummings (YV p. 52)
Ten Little Christmas Trees   R. Bennett (*Book of a Thousand Poems* p. 546)

Songs   O Christmas Tree, O Christmas Tree (*Carol, gaily carol* no. 41)
Christmas Trees (*Sing a Song* 1.44)

Prayers 58, 59

Activities   Make four Christmas tree friezes hung with presents that Dads, Mums, babies and the children would like using pictures cut from magazines and catalogues. Make mobiles of cut-out Christmas trees. Study different kinds of pine and fir trees. Decorate your Christmas tree.

Clothes

Theme   Clothes are what we have to wear every day. We wear different clothes for different kinds of weather. There are special clothes for special times—rain clothes, play clothes, sunbathing, gym clothes, party clothes, school uniforms, pyjamas, etc. Some people wear uniforms to show who they are e.g. policeman, school-crossing lady, nurse, soldier, bus conductor, jockey, etc. Some people wear clothes to protect them. Clothes are made from different materials—wool, cotton, nylon, etc. We fasten our clothes in different ways using buttons, zips, toggles, etc. Long ago people wore different clothes. In other countries the clothes are different too.

Stories   The Young Man and the Swallow p. 171
Joseph's Coat of Many Colours (*Genesis* 37)
The Emperor's New Clothes (*Together Today* p. 166)

Poems   Tailor   E. Farjeon (S&D p. 93)
Mummy has scissors (S&D p. 94)
John   N. M. Bodecker (*Funny Rhymes* p. 12)
In my new clothing   H. G. Henderson (*Funny Rhymes* p. 98)
Hark, hark, the Dogs do Bark   Nursery Rhyme

Songs   When I get dressed (*Over & Over* p. 76)
Mister Banjo (*Okki* no. 30)
My hat it has three colours (*Okki* no. 48)
The clown (*Apusskidu* no. 35)

Prayers 52, 67

Activities   Hold a fancy-dress parade. Collect pictures of uniforms and identify what jobs the people do. Design some fashions of your own. Make a collage using various materials. Sort clothes into sets and pairs. Study the symmetry of clothes shapes. Look at historical costumes from pictures or a local museum.

Colours

Theme   There are colours all around us. What are the four primary colours? The fun of mixing paints, choosing and making colours. In nature each season has different colours. Some colours are clear to see, like black and white. Others are not easy to see—some animals use camouflage, so do soldiers. What are your favourite colours? Light is made up of all the colours. Sometimes you can see this in a rainbow—what are the seven colours of the rainbow? (Red, orange, yellow, green, blue, indigo and violet.) When might you see a rainbow? The rainbow we sometimes see in the sky after rain is caused by sunlight being refracted by the raindrops. Sometimes you see rainbow colours in a bubble.

Stories   Noah's Ark (*Genesis* 6)
Joseph and his coat of many colours (*Genesis* 37)

Poems   Colours   Christina Rossetti (YP p. 68, *Fancy Free* p. 74)
Colour   Anon (*Book of a Thousand Poems* p. 301)
What is Red?   M. O'Neil (*Rhyme Time* p. 19)

Songs   Yellow Submarine (*Apusskidu* no 4)
Sing a Rainbow (*Apusskidu* no. 5)
Who put the colours in a rainbow? (CP no. 12)
O Lovely World of Colour (NCS 23)

Prayers 56, 61, 65, 66

Activities   Refract the sun's rays through a glass prism to see the rainbow colours. Investigate the mixing of colours. Set up a colour table, see how many shades of one colour you can find. Display pictures which show camouflage in nature. Make a graph of favourite colours. Paint a rainbow.

Communications

Theme   There are many ways of 'talking' to people. We can speak to them with our voices e.g. whispering, shouting. We can write a letter or send a telegram. We can use the telephone. If people can see us we can use a sign or signal e.g. waving, semaphore, smoke signals. We can also send messages without words using secret codes, morse code, flags or lights. People who are deaf and dumb communicate by sign language. There are many ways, too, in which people communicate with us—the written word in books and newspapers, the spoken word through radio, television, records and tapes. We can talk to people on the other side of the world. In our prayers we are talking to God.

Stories   The Ten Commandments (*Exodus* 20)
The Writing on the Wall (*Daniel* 3)
Tulsi the Peacemaker (*Together Today* p. 252)
A newspaper story ...

Poems   The Radio Men   E. Jennings (B&P)
Newspaper   A. Horrox (S&D p. 95)
Newspapers   Anon (S&D p. 98)

Songs   Kum ba yah (SSL no. 23)
The ink is black, the page is white (SSL no. 39)

Prayers 26, 50, 65

Activities   Write letters to each other, to friends and families. Set up a pillar box, post office, and postmen to collect, sort and deliver. Collect postage stamps and stamped envelopes and study postmarks. Display local and national newspapers. Produce your own school, class or group newspaper. Create your own radio or television programme. Investigate the telephone, dialling and telephone directories. Mime signals, actions, people's jobs, etc. and guess the message.

Creation

Theme   Every day we are able to create something new. We can create happiness and laughter in other people, or sadness and sorrow. We can create stories with our imagination through speaking or writing. We can create something through acting, music and movement. We can create pictures and models. We can create ideas through our thinking. At home families are being created by husbands and wives having and caring for their children. There are many stories about the creation of the world. The Bible tells us that God took six days to create the world and rested on the seventh day. We can use the raw materials supplied by God to create a better world.

Stories   The Creation (*Genesis* 1)

Poems   Creation (*Sing, Say and Move* p. 26)
In the Beginning   A. P. Dixon (S&D p. 20)
Who?   J. Cattermull (FPB p. 123, *Full Swing* p. 112)

Songs   Morning has Broken (MHB 62)
God who made the earth (CP no. 10)
Who put the colours in the rainbow? (CP no. 12)
He made me (CP no. 18)

Prayers   40, 45, 61, 65, 68

Activities   Create a frieze showing the Biblical version of creation. Read other myths and legends about the creation of the world. Discuss the scientific view of evolution—show pictures of erupting volcanoes to show the origin of earth's land forms (pumice stone is volcanic rock) grow the earliest plants—algae—by keeping pond water in a jar till it goes green. (See also Dinosaurs p. 44) Provide an opportunity for each child to display something of their own creation.

Danger!—Safety First

Theme   Children get hurt in accidents every day both at home and when they are out and about. What are the dangers at home? Never play near a *fire*. What should you do if a fire starts? The dangers of burning and scalding. Beware of electric plugs. Do not touch *medicines*, they may be poisonous. Can you tell the difference between sweets and pills. If an accident happened at home how could you get help?

On the road do you know the Green Cross Code? When you are out, where is it safe to play? Beware of roads, building sites, railway lines, ponds, rivers, canals. What dangers are there at the seaside? There are also dangers at school—what accidents do you know about? Could they have been avoided? Remember—safety first.

Stories   The Lost Sheep p. 147
Jesus is lost and found (*Luke* 2.40)
Topsy and Tim go safely   J & G Anderson (Holmes McDougal)
Topsy and Tim take no risks   J & G Anderson (Holmes McDougal)

Poems   Selected Cautionary Verses   H. Belloc (Puffin)

Songs   The fireman (*Apusskidu* no. 33)
If I had a hammer (SSL no. 37)

Prayers 19, 32, 49, 50, 63, 67, 70

Activities   Study the work of people who help save others from danger—police (and their dogs), lifeboatmen, helicopter crews, mountain rescue teams, firemen, etc. Check the children know common symbols and words for danger—poisons, electricity, etc. Tape record some 'dangerous sounds' e.g. fire crackling, kettle boiling, bottle breaking. Design simple safety first posters. Act out telephoning in an emergency. Collect containers of safe and unsafe contents. Write off to ROSPA, 1 Grosvenor Crescent, London SW1, for safety first material.

Refer to: *Road Sense, Home Safety, Water Safety, First Aid* (Ladybird Series)

Dinosaurs

Theme   Fossil remains of animals and plants have been buried under the ground for millions of years. Scientists have found fossil bones of animals called dinosaurs. Dinosaurs lived on earth long before man. Some dinosaurs were enormous, but many were not much larger than us. Do you know the names of any dinosaurs? All the dinosaurs eventually died out but no one really knows why. Today there are no dinosaurs, but some animals are rather like dinosaurs e.g. the tortoise, crocodile and rhinoceros. You can find out more about dinosaurs from books, museums and parks. See what you can find out.

Stories   Mary and her Bones p. 151
Desmond the Dinosaur   A. Braithwaite (Dinosaur)
Danny and the Dinosaur   S. Hoff (World's Work)
Monster series (Longman's Breakthrough series)
Dinosaurs and all that rubbish   M. Foreman (Hamish Hamilton)

Poems   Animal Life   Tom Stanier (*Watch* p. 9)
So Big!   M. Fatchen (*Amazing Monsters* p. 64)
Hocus Pocus Diplodocus   Tom Stanier (Macdonald)
Oh Dinosaur   B. Ireson (Corgi/Carousel)
Dinosaurs and beasts of yore   W. Cole (Collins)

Songs   The Prehistoric Animal Brigade (Okki no. 8)
Dem Dry Bones (*Watch* p. 4)

Prayer 54

Activities   Draw or make models of dinosaurs and set them in a pop-up picture landscape. Draw dinosaur skeletons, white on black, and dinosaur footprints. Measure and draw a life-size dinosaur. Construct a mobile of flying creatures. Make up rhythms for dinosaur names. Study modern reptiles, observe a tortoise or lizard. Imagine a newly discovered dinosaur, draw or paint it and make up a name for it. Find out about the Loch Ness monster. Collect and study fossils.
Movement theme—dinosaurs on the move!

Dragons

Theme   What is a dragon? In the past people believed there were huge and fearful monsters called dragons. They were usually green, like a snake or a crocodile. They could live on land, in the sea, or in the air for they had wings like a bat. They could also breathe fire. In China dragons were thought to be good, but in other lands they were evil, bad creatures. There are many stories of brave men like St George who killed dragons. Today nobody fights dragons, for we know there are no such animals. But there are still bad things, like dragons, inside each of us that we have to fight. These are the 'dragons' which make us mean and angry, greedy and selfish. Do you think there are any of these dragons inside you?

Stories   St George and the Dragon (*Together Today* p. 228)
The Dragon's Teeth (*Together Today* p. 165)
The Laughing Dragon   R. Wilson (TMAS p. 219)
Dragons   C. Rawson (Usborne Story Books)

Poems   A Small Dragon   B. Patten (*Amazing Monster* p. 20)
The Dragon with a big nose   K. Henderson (RAS p. 50)
Dragon Smoke   L. Moore (WGMM p. 94)
A Knight and a Lady   Anon (YP p. 137)
The Dragon   M. Mullineaux (CFM p. 25)

Songs   Maggon, the bad tempered dragon (*Apusskidu* no. 55)
Chinatown Dragon (*Harlequin* no. 24)
Puff the Magic Dragon (*Sing a Song* I no. 8)

Prayers 10, 22

Activities   Make a large collage of a dragon using eggboxes painted green, for example. Construct a Chinese dragon using a papier mâché head and material for the body. Perform a dragon dance. Collect pictures of dragons e.g. Viking dragon boats, Welsh dragon, gargoyles, etc. Study how lizards are like dragons.
(See also Chinese New Year, p. 34)

Easter

Theme   Easter falls somewhere between 22nd March and 25th April, on the first Sunday following a full moon in spring. It is the most important Christian festival. *Palm Sunday*, the Sunday before Easter Sunday marks the beginning of Holy Week. On Palm Sunday we remember the entry of Jesus into Jerusalem riding on a donkey. In some churches children are given small palm crosses on this day. *Maundy Thursday* is the day when Christians remember the Last Supper which Jesus shared with his disciples. At this meal Jesus washed the feet of his disciples. He blessed the bread and wine, telling the disciples that whenever they ate or drank bread and wine in the future they should remember him. *Good Friday* is the day when Christians remember the death of Jesus on the cross. It is a national holiday, and many people eat hot cross buns on this day.

Easter Sunday is when we celebrate the day that Christ rose from the dead, churches are made pretty with spring flowers and new candles are lit. It is also the day when chocolate Easter eggs are given.

The name Easter comes from that of Eostre, Goddess of the Dawn, whose spring festival occured at the vernal equinox when day and night were of equal length. It is also the time of the Jewish Passover feast, held to give thanks for the escape of the Israelites from Egypt.

The Easter Story

> The Entry into Jerusalem (*Mark* 11.1, *Luke* 19.29, *Matt.* 21)
> Jesus cleanses the Temple (*Luke* 19.45)
> Judas plots to betray Jesus (*Matt.* 26)
> The Last Supper (*Mark* 14.12, *John* 13)
> Jesus is arrested (*Matt.* 26.47)
> Peter denies Jesus (*Matt.* 26.69)
> Jesus before Pontius Pilate (*Matt.* 27.19)
> The Crucifixion (*Matt.* 27.27)
> The Resurrection (*John* 20.1)
> Thomas doubts Jesus (*John* 20.24)

Easter Customs

Theme   Where did our Easter customs come from?

Easter eggs   The eating of eggs used to be forbidden during Lent, but at the end of Lent they were coloured and given as presents. Egg-rolling games were also played, in memory of the stone being rolled away from the tomb of Jesus. A game like conkers using hard-boiled eggs held in the hand was also played. Eggs are symbols of the resurrection and the promise of new life.

Hot cross buns   Buns with crosses on them, and flavoured with spices, were specially made to be eaten on Good Friday.

Easter bunny   The Easter rabbit was originally a hare which was sacred to the goddess Eostre.

Simnel cakes   were traditionally given to mothers on Mothering Sunday and kept to be eaten at Easter. They were spicy cakes topped with almond paste with eleven almond 'eggs' representing the apostles (minus Judas).

Royal Maundy   Every Maundy Thursday the Queen gives special coins in coloured leather purses to a group of old age pensioners. There is one pensioner for each year of the Queen's life. In the old days the monarch would wash the feet of the poor, in memory of the time Jesus washed his disciples' feet at the Last Supper.

Easter bonnets   Easter is a time of processions, and at some parades there is an Easter bonnet competition where people wear funny hats which they have made for themselves.

Stories   The Mark on the Donkey (*Together Today* p. 203)
The Easter Lamb   M. Gore (TMAS p. 89)
Easter Chickens   E. Colwell (*Time for a Story* p. 33)

Poems   He is risen   C. F. Alexander (*Times Delights* p. 94)

Songs   Lord of the Dance (SSL no. 29)
Hurray for Jesus (SSL no. 50)
We have a King who rides a donkey (SSL no. 51)
Hot Cross Buns (ONS p. 18)

Prayers 7, 12, 17, 42, 62, 63

Activities   Have a Palm Sunday type procession, with palm-shaped leaves made from sugar paper, singing Hosanna and praises, or an Easter hymn. Make palm crosses from dried rushes. Create an Easter garden with mosses and small plants in a tray of earth, raised into a mound in one corner with three crosses, and another mound with a round stone pressed in front. Hold a decorated egg competition or display. Try dyeing eggs by boiling them in spinach (green), beetroot (red), onions skins (orange/brown), etc. Cook some hot cross buns, a Simnel cake, or Easter bunny biscuits. Make Easter presents or give eggs in decorated boxes to local old people. Make Easter cards to take home. Hold a parade of home-made Easter bonnets.

Refer to: *The Easter Book* (Macdonald)

Easter Biscuits

225 g self-raising flour	a little grated lemon rind
pinch of salt	50 g currants
100 g butter or margarine	1 egg
100 g sugar	

Sift together the flour and the salt. Rub in the fat. Add the sugar, lemon rind and currants and stir in the beaten egg. Knead lightly on a floured board and roll out to about 6 mm thick. Cut into rounds with a fluted cutter and place on greased baking trays. Bake for 15 minutes 180°C, Gas mark 4. This will make about 30 biscuits.

Eggs

Theme   Wild birds lay eggs in the spring months, but farm hens lay eggs all through the year. Eggs are full of goodness to eat. Many people eat eggs for breakfast. Eggs are usually graded according to weight and size—there are seven sizes numbered 1–7. Which size egg do you eat at home? Eggs are sold by the dozen or half dozen. How many is that? There are many ways to cook an egg. When boiling an egg some people use egg timers. The two parts of an egg are the yolk and the white. If it was fertilised and kept warm the yolk would grow into a baby chick and hatch after twenty-one days. Eggs are very fragile. If you ever find eggs in a nest you should leave them alone. Eggs contain the beginning of new life.

Stories   The Goose that laid the Golden Eggs p. 135
The Ugly Duckling (*Together Today* p. 257)

Poems   Hen's Song   R. Fyleman (WGMM p. 116)
Eggs are laid by Turkeys   M. A. Hoberman (WGMM p. 117)
Three Little Chickens   Anon (*Rhyme Time* p. 132)

Song   Higgledy Piggledy My Black Hen   Trad.

Prayers 15, 66

Activities   Make egg heads by painting or drawing eggshells and glueing on hair or hats. Mobiles can be made by hanging coloured eggshells from coathangers. Make mosaics from broken eggshells. Study birds eggs, their variety and size. Test eggs for freshness (fresh eggs sink in salt water, old eggs float). Weigh eggs of different sizes. Hold an egg-and-spoon race.
    (See also Birds p. 17)

49

Fathers

Theme   A father is a very special person in a family. It takes a father and a mother to make a baby child. Most children have a father at home to love and care for them. Fathers are usually big and strong. Like mothers, fathers are interested in helping the children to grow up and to learn many things. Fathers often go out to work to provide a home for mother and children. In the animal world fathers often go hunting for food, and sometimes take it in turn to guard the young ones. We talk about God as our father because he loves and cares for his whole family throughout the world.

Stories   The Bundle of Sticks p. 121
The Miller, the Son and the Donkey p. 154
Abraham and Isaac (*Genesis* 17)

Poems   Dads   B. Ireson (*Over & Over Again* p. 68)
Father says   M. Rosen (FPB p. 12)
When Dad felt bad   C. Causley (FPB p. 36)
Dad and the cat and the tree   K. Wright (*Funny Rhymes* p. 32)

Songs   Dance to your Daddy (ONS p. 69)
We're going home (SSL no. 59)
When Father papered the Parlour (*Apusskidu* no. 34)
At half past three we go home to tea (SSL no. 58)
Daddy wouldn't buy me a bow-wow (*Apusskidu* no. 43)

Prayers 25, 44, 67

Activities   Paint a picture of Dad, or an uncle in your family. Make a family folder of stories and pictures. Make a card or small gift for Father's Day. Display pictures of families around the world. Study animal families.

Favourite Things

Theme   We all have favourite things. Favourite colour, smell, toy, flower, sound, game, place, animal, story, etc. We hope or wish for our favourite things to happen; that we can go on a special outing, or that we'll be given something special, or that something nice will happen to someone we love. Some old stories have fairies which grant three wishes. What would your wishes be? When people pray they often tell God about their hopes and wishes.

Stories   The Three Wishes (*Together Today* p. 247)
              Your favourite story . . .

Poems   Things I like   M. H. Greenfield (CFM p. 34)
             Shining Things   E. Gould (CFM p. 170, *Full Swing* p. 110)

Songs   These are a few of my favourite things (*The Sound of Music*)
             Doh a Deer (*The Sound of Music*)
             Glad that I live am I (MHB 61)

Prayers 13, 45, 57, 65

Activities   Display favourite toys (or pictures of them). Make a graph of favourite colours or animals. Write about your favourite place—beach, playground, park, home, etc. Make a scrapbook of favourite things. Talk about the wishes you have for yourself, other people, and for the world. Draw or paint your favourite meal, game, song, clothes, story, etc.

Feet

Theme Feet are important parts of your body. Do you know why? You need feet to stand up, to walk, to run and to play on. A foot is made up of twenty-six different bones, and is arched to help you balance. Your toes help to grip the floor. If you were a monkey you would swing on a branch with your toes! Feet need looking after—we must remember to keep our toenails cut, to keep our feet clean, and to wear comfortable shoes. A child's foot is growing all the time—do you know what size shoe you take? Special shoes are needed for different occasions e.g. plimsolls, boots, slippers. Animal feet include claws, paws, hooves, and flippers. Sometimes you can see the footprints or tracks of animals. People who are Christians try to follow in the footsteps of Christ.

Stories Jesus washes his disciples' feet (*John* 12:3)
The Elves and the Shoemaker   Trad. (Ladybird)
The Story of the Five Toes   R. Bamberger (*First Story Book* p. 11)

Poems Feet   I. Thompson (CFM p. 30)
Can you walk on tiptoe   Anon (S&D p. 104)
Jump or Jiggle   E. Beyer
Choosing Shoes   F. Wolfe (*Rhyme Time* p. 163)
Pins and Needles   P. Clarke (*Funny Rhymes* p. 107)

Songs I danced in the morning (SSL no. 29)
Games to play with feet (TLP p. 139)
Dance to your Daddy (*Over & Over* p. 162)
Marching Songs

Prayers 30, 32, 43

Activities Make a collage of feet by drawing round and colouring foot shapes. Measure feet. Make a graph of shoe sizes. Study animal and bird tracks. Display various kinds of shoes. Sorting quiz—which foot matches which animal?
Movement themes—hopping, stepping, skipping, walking on tiptoe, pigeon steps, etc.

Fireworks

Theme   5th November is the anniversary of the Gunpowder Plot. On that day in 1605 a man called Guy Fawkes was caught trying to blow up the Houses of Parliament with gunpowder. Ever since, on 5th November people have made guys, large models of Guy Fawkes, to burn on bonfires, and let off fireworks. Fireworks are pretty to watch but they are dangerous. They can burn you or blow up in someone's face. Remember the Firework Code. Fires are useful, in the home for cooking and heating, in factories for furnaces, in space for rocket engines, but fire can be dangerous, too. In the home beware of matches, burns and scalds. The need for fire guards. Talk about the fire service—their work and the dangers involved.

Stories   Why the Robin has a Red Breast p. 169
How Prometheus brought fire to man (*Together Today* p. 188)
I am a Fire   J. Taylor (Blackwell)
Elijah and the Fire (*I Kings* 18)
Daniel in the Fire (*Daniel* 3)

Poems   November the Fifth   L. Clark (YP p. 72)
Fireworks   J. Reeves (HL p. 78)
Bonfire Night   R. Brighton (SS p. 24)
Please to Remember the Fifth of November . . .   Trad.
Fire   J. Reeves (*The Wandering Moon*, Heinemann)
Fire Down Below (*The Swinging Rainbow* p. 19)

Songs   The fireman (*Apusskidu* no. 33)
Light up the Fire (CP no. 55)
London's Burning (ONS p. 18)

Prayers 47, 60, 67

Activities   Make a guy by stuffing old stockings to make legs, arms and body, dress in old clothes and use a mask for a face. Paint a firework frieze using luminescent paint on a black background. Investigate how rockets work. Act out the Guy Fawkes story. Find out about the Great Fire of London. Study the work of the fire service. Discuss school fire drill—show bells, fire doors, fire extinguishers. Look out for yellow fire hydrant signs. Fire needs air—put a jam jar over a burning candle.

Flowers

Theme Everyone likes flowers. They are beautiful to look at, and some are lovely to smell. People grow flowers in gardens and greenhouses, or in pots indoors. Flowers grow from seeds, and then the flower is where new seeds are made. Some flowers, like tulips and daffodils, grow from bulbs. Wild flowers grow on roadsides and sunny banks. Look at them but do not pick them, because if the flowers are picked the plant cannot make new seeds and no more plants can grow. Flowers produce a sweet juice called nectar, bees and butterflies collect it and while they do so they spread pollen to other flowers. Many people have favourite flowers—which do you like best?

Stories Lilies of the Field (*Luke* 12.27)
The Forgotten Treasure (*Together Today* p. 240)
The Stolen Tulips (*Together Today* p. 240)
Snow-white and Rose-red   Trad.

Poems A Watering Rhyme   P. A. Ropes (CFM p. 36)

Songs Think of a world without any flowers (SSL no. 15)
All the flowers are waking (SSL no. 48)
All Things Bright and Beautiful (MHB 57)
Mary, Mary, quite contrary (ONS p. 6)

Prayers 5, 27, 38, 53, 61, 65

Activities Study the flowers in a flower shop, nursery, park, wood or garden. Make tissue paper flowers. Create a collage of some spring flowers. Study flower catalogues and display reference books. Plant a seed or bulb and keep a record of its growth. Show how growing plants need water, soil, light and air. Use a flower press to press and mount some wild flowers. Make a pot-pourri of summer scents using dried rose petals, herbs, etc.

Forgiving

Theme   Sometimes we get upset by other people. They say things which are not very nice. They do things which upset us and hurt us— sometimes they are spiteful and bad tempered. We should try to forgive them, especially if they say 'sorry'. When we say sorry we are asking someone to forgive us. There is much more to being sorry than just saying sorry. Being sorry means that we know we have done wrong and we want to make the other person feel better. Forgiving people is part of loving them. Jesus said that God loves each one of us, and forgives all who are truly sorry.

Stories   Joseph and his brothers (*Genesis* 37)
           The unmerciful servant (*Matt.* 18)
           The Prodigal Son (*Luke.* 15)

Poems   The Quarrel   E. Farjeon (FPB p. 26)

Songs   At half past three we go home to tea (SSL no. 58)
           Think, think on these things (SSL 38)

Prayers 1, 7, 9, 10, 11, 12, 46, 69

Activities   Discuss the times when we ought to feel and say sorry. Paint pictures of faces—happy faces and sad faces. Have a 'Smile' campaign in class or school. Act out one of the Bible stories from the story section above. Mime a quarrel and how it is settled. Learn what the Lord's Prayer says about forgiving.

Friends and Neighbours

Theme   What is a friend? Usually they are people who like the same
things and share the same interests. Life can be very lonely without friends.
It is important to be a good friend as well as to have good friends. A good
friend is someone who shares what he has, and helps others when he can.
There is an old saying 'A friend in need is a friend indeed'. Neighbours are
people who live near us, in our neighbourhood. They too should be our
friends. When you have friends and neighbours the whole world is a happier
place.

Stories   How Jane found Friends p. 138
The Good Samaritan (*Luke* 10)
David and Jonathan (*I Samuel* 20)
How the Owl Became   T. Hughes (from *How the Whale
Became* Puffin)
The Bear that Spoke (*Together Today* p. 143)

Poems   A Thank You for Friends   Rodney Bennett (*Book of a
Thousand Poems* p. 512)

Songs   Jesus friend of little children (MHB no. 37)
When I needed a neighbour (CP no. 65, SSL no. 35)
Look out for loneliness (SSL no. 36)
Think, think on these things (SSL no. 38)
The ink is black, the page is white (SSL no. 39)
There's a friend for little children (MHB no. 5)

Prayers   21, 24, 29, 44, 67, 69

Activities   Paint or draw pictures of friends. Write a description of your
friend—see if others recognise who the friend is. Think of some ways of
being friendly to people in your neighbourhood e.g. local old people's
home. Talk about animal friends such as guide dogs. How do animals show
they are friendly?

Gardens

Theme   A garden is a place for growing plants and flowers. When God made the world it is said that he first planted a garden—the Garden of Eden. It can be fun growing things, but it is also hard work. Gardens must be weeded and watered, grass must be cut, and plants cared for. There are gardens of all kinds. A window box, tub or hanging basket can be a small garden. Gardens are not only for growing things, gardens are for sitting in, playing in, and for hanging up the washing. If you have a garden it is nice to share with others what you have grown.

Stories   The Discontented Pig p. 124
A Little Gardening   E. Roberts (*More Stories to Tell* p. 41)
The Garden of Eden (*Genesis* 2)

Poems   Mary, Mary, quite contrary   Trad.
Johnny Crow's Garden (*A Golden Land* p. 66)
In the Garden (*This Little Puffin* p. 41–48)
In my Garden   Anon (CFM p. 44)

Songs   The flowers that grow in the garden (SSL no. 53)
One potato, two potato (*Apusskidu* no. 31)
Katie's garden (*Apusskidu* no. 50)
Somebody greater (CP no. 5)
When God made the garden of creation (CP no. 16)
In our dear Lord's garden (MHB no. 60)

Prayers 27, 38, 65, 68

Activities   Grow a herb garden with seeds e.g. parsley, thyme and cuttings e.g. sage and rosemary. Plant various flower seeds. Sow peas, beans, sunflower seeds, corn. Make a miniature garden in trays or boxes using moss, violets, daisies, clover, cactus, etc. (An imitation pond can be made from a mirror). Cultivate miniature trees using pips or seeds e.g. oranges and apples. Visit a local garden or park.

Gifts

Theme   There are special times for giving and receiving presents. Why do we give them? To show we love and care for someone. We have to choose the present to suit the person. If you had to choose a gift for Mummy, Daddy, Grandma or your best friend what would it be? Giving and receiving (saying thank you for the presents we receive). Making presents. Some things we give cannot be touched or seen—helping someone, doing a job, cheering someone up, finding something that is lost. At Christmas we use gifts to remember the gifts given by the Wise Men to the baby Jesus.

Stories   St Nicholas and the Gifts p. 162
The Wise Men bring gifts (*Matt.* 2)
The Widow's Mite (*Luke* 21)
The Rich Man and the Beggar (*Luke* 16)
The Bishop's Candlesticks (*Together Today* p. 149)

Poems   All good gifts around us
Are sent from heaven above,
Then thank the Lord, O thank the Lord,
For all His love.
                                        J. M. Campbell

Songs   Simple gifts (FFC p. 19)
The best gift (CP no. 59)
The wise may bring their learning (CP no. 64)
Here we come with gladness (MHB no. 56)
The first day of Christmas (*Carol Gaily Carol* no. 42)

Prayers 5, 33, 39, 41

Activities   Wrap up some surprise gifts the children have made. Make a frieze of your favourite gifts. Design some gift wrapping paper or gift tags. Write or talk about 'My favourite present'.

Gold

Theme   Gold is a metal sometimes found in rocks. It is also a colour.
Wedding rings are usually gold. Other metals like brass are a golden colour.
What else can you think of that is golden—sand, sunshine, ripe corn, hair...?
Sweets are sometimes wrapped in gold paper. Thread and tinsel can be
gold. Sovereigns are gold coins. Some people think that gold is the most
valuable thing in the world. What is your most valuable thing? Would you
swap it for gold?

Stories   The Goose that laid the Golden Eggs p. 135
            The Jar of Ants p. 142
            Midas and the Golden Touch (*Together Today* p. 206)
            Salt is Better than Gold (*Together Today* p. 233)
            Atalanta (ibid p. 141)
            The Golden Calf (*Exodus* 32)
            Rumpelstiltskin (spinning straw into gold)   Grimm

Poems   Golden glories   Christina Rossetti (*Full Swing* p. 115)
            Golden Hair   James Joyce (CFM p. 188)

Songs   Daisies are our Silver (MHB no. 63)

Prayers 65, 68

Activities   Try shining some old pennies to make them look like gold.
Show how to spin a coin. Can the children guess whether it will come down
heads or tails? Act out one of the stories, illustrate it with pictures or get
children to tell it in their own words. Make a colour table collection of gold
pictures and objects. Study a goldfish, goldfinch, golden eagle, golden
labrador or a golden pheasant. Where can you see something golden in your
neighbourhood?

Good Health

Theme   What helps to keep you strong and healthy? The need for food, exercise, rest and loving care. The body needs food for growth and energy. It is important to have a good breakfast. Exercise is important in making bodies strong and keeping them in good working order. Exercise helps to develop healthy muscles. What is your favourite form of exercise? We need rest, muscles get tired. We need lots of sleep to help our bodies grow quickly. When we are older we can go to bed later. What do you feel like in the morning if you go to bed late? We need loving care from adults who work for us, look after us when we are ill, cook our food, wash our clothes, etc. How you can help to keep healthy—washing and cleaning teeth. The habits of good health.

Stories   Elisha heals the leper (*II Kings* 5)
Jesus heals the leper (*Mark* 1.40)
Jesus restores Jairus' daughter (*Mark* 5.22)
The Invalid at the Pool (*John* 5.2)
The Mirror of Truth (*Together Today* p. 207)

Poems   As Fit as a Fiddle   P. Clarke (YP p. 48)
Sneezing   Anon (YP p. 45)
Measles   K. Hadden (*Big Dipper* p. 39)

Songs   For all the strength we have (SSL no. 16)
O Jesus we are well and strong (SSL no. 40)
If you're happy (*Apusskidu* no. 1)
One finger, one thumb keep moving (*Okki* no. 46)
I think I've caught a cold (*Harlequin* no. 34)

Prayers 17, 27, 66

Activities   Make a frieze showing foods that are good for the body. Collect and mount labels and wrappers of healthy foods. Make a chart of the different diseases the children have had. Study how disease is spread. Acting—doctors and nurses, life in hospital.
   (See also Teeth p. 108)

Halloween

Theme   Many years ago people believed that witches rode their broomsticks across the moon on 31st October. It was All Hallows Eve, which we call Halloween. As well as broomsticks witches were supposed to have black cats and big cauldrons in which they mixed their magic spells. It is what we call a superstition. A superstition is something people believe in which is not true. What other superstitions are there? What number is supposed to be unlucky?

Stories   It's Halloween   Jack Prelutsky (World's Work 1977)
Witches   C. Rawson (Usborne Story Books)
Judy and the Fairy Cat   E. Colwell (*More Stories to Tell* p. 70)

Poems   Halloween   L. Clark (*Times Delights* p. 101)
Witches' Spells   A. Nightingale (SS p. 63)
The Witch   P. H. Ilott (CFM p. 187)
W is for Witch   E. Farjeon (S&D p. 20)

Songs   There was an old witch (*Apusskidu* no. 17)
Gobbolino, the witch's cat (*Apusskidu* no. 53)
The witch's broomstick (*Over and Over* p. 200)
Halloween's coming (*Harlequin* no. 35)
Spooky (*Harlequin* no. 36)

Prayers 22, 63, 67

Activities   A Halloween dance of witches, ghosts, skeletons, cats and bats. Make a Halloween frieze and mobiles of flying witches. Construct black conical hats and halloween masks. Have a Halloween party, with a fancy dress parade and games like apple bobbing or passing the orange under chins.

Hands

Theme   Hands come in pairs—who knows their right from their left hand? Hands are used for work and play, for holding and for feeling—the sense of touch. We can feel if things are rough or smooth, hot or cold, heavy or light. We can tell the feel of things without looking. Hands are for holding, throwing, catching, carrying, dressing, tying, wiping, washing, writing, painting, pushing, pulling, stroking, picking, planting, etc. The shape of our hands. The parts of the hand—palms, fingernails, joints, knuckles. Some people are born without hands, or become crippled. Artificial hands can be fitted. Some people without hands can become artists by using their feet or mouths. We should be grateful for having our hands. And they should also be used to help others both in school and at home.

Stories   Five Little Fingers p. 129
Feeling the Elephant (*Together Today* p. 170)
The Story of the Five Fingers   R. Bamberger (*My First Big Story Book* p. 31)
Jesus healed many sick people by touching them with his hands
        The leper (*Matt.* 8.2)
        Jairus' daughter (*Luke* 8.41)
        Malchus' Ear (*Luke* 22.49)
        The man with a withered hand (*Matt.* 12.10)

Poems   Hands   Peter Young (FPB p. 9)
This is the Hand   M. Rosen (FPB p. 8)

Songs   Hands to work and feet to run (SSL no. 21)
Jesus' hands were kind hands (SSL no. 33)
He's got the whole world in his hands (CP no. 19)

Prayers 29, 30, 35, 43, 48

Activities   Play some hand games; ask the children to pat their heads and rub their tummies at the same time. Or clasp hands with fingers interlocked; can they raise whichever finger is pointed to? Make finger paintings and printing. Play with glove puppets and a puppet theatre. Set up a 'touching corner' with interesting things to touch and talk about. Investigate hand signals—anger, greeting, informing. Road and police signals. Measuring with the hands, and measuring hands.

Happiness

Theme   If you are feeling happy show it with a smile. Happiness spreads happiness, but the opposite it also true. What are the ways of making other people happy? How do you know if someone is happy? Animals show happiness in different ways—wagging tails, purring, etc. Laughing is one way of showing happiness. What makes you laugh? Some stories have happy endings. Some music is happy. What do people do to show they are happy—smile, clap, cheer, jump for joy?

Stories   The Shirt of Happiness p. 164
Mr Happy (Mr Grumpy)   R. Hargreaves (Thurman)
Everything's Horrid Today   A. Stadon (*More Stories to Tell* p. 90)
Cross-Patch   M. Baker (TMAS p. 244)
How Diogenes found Happiness (*Together Today* p. 186)

Poems   Days   P. Larkin (*Bits and Pieces*)
Happiness   A. A. Milne (*Rhyme Time* p. 107)

The world is so full of a number of things,
I'm sure we should all be as happy as kings
R. L. Stevenson

Songs   If you're happy (*Apusskidu* no. 1)
O Lord! Shout for Joy (SSL no. 4)
Lord, I love to stamp and shout (SSL no. 5)
The clown (*Apusskidu* no. 35)

Prayers 5, 7, 8, 19, 23, 51

Activities   Try drawing faces which are happy, sad, angry, crying, smiling, laughing. Act pulling funny faces, and doing funny walks. Do a survey of 'Things which make us happy' and 'Things which make us unhappy'. Talk about a time when you made someone feel happy, and when you made someone feel unhappy.

Harvest Festival

Theme   In September there are celebrations all over the country in schools and churches to celebrate the Harvest Home. Churches are made beautiful with flowers and sheaves of corn. Both children and adults bring small gifts of fruit and vegetables to the Harvest Festival. Sometimes dolls are made by plaiting strands of corn together. In olden days the 'dolly' represented the Corn Goddess and was kept to ensure a good harvest for the following year.

Stories   Jesus Feeds the Five Thousand (*Matt.* 14:15)
The Strange Treasure (*Together Today* p. 241)
The Trolls Share (*Together Today* p. 250)
The Story of Ruth (*Ruth* 1)
The Story of Joseph (*Genesis* 37)

Poems   Oats and Beans and Barley   Action poem (HL p. 35)
Harvest Song   Anon (CFM p. 86)

Songs   Find a trolley (NCS 38)
First the seed (NCS 24)
When the corn is planted (SSL no. 55)
We plough the fields and scatter (NCS 93)
Harvest (*Harlequin* no. 31)

Prayers 27, 39, 40, 52, 65, 66, 68

Activities   Make a frieze showing food from the earth, the trees and the sea. Compile a graph of favourite foods. Visit a market, dairy farm or supermarket. Display a collection of corn dollies. Use lengths of straw to make pictures or patterns, fix pieces together to form stars. Try printing with different vegetables, or make vegetable animals using matchsticks, drawing pins, etc.

Hobbies and Games

Theme   People do different things to enjoy themselves when they are
not working. Some play games, others watch TV, read, sew, knit, make
things, collect things, dance or do sports. What do you do in your spare
time? What games do you like playing? Some people like to collect things.
Collecting can be fun. Some collections, like stamps and coins, can be
worth a lot of money. What sort of things do people collect? Grown-ups
sometimes have hobbies—do your Mum and Dad have hobbies? Perhaps
they would come to school to talk about it.

Stories   James and his Machines p. 141
         The Girl who liked watching Stars p. 133
         Mary and her Bones p. 151

Poems   My Brother Bert   T. Hughes (RAS p. 78)
         Song for a Ball-game   W. Thorley (RAS p. 64)
         Skipping Rhymes (RAS p. 38)
         Johnny's Pockets   A. Winn (YP p. 37)

Songs   Girls and Boys come out to Play (ONS p. 64)
         What shall we do when we all go out (TLP p. 179)

Prayers 41, 53, 57

Activities   Make a graph or diagram of games children like best.
Display things they have made, ask children to talk about how they made
them. Collect pictures of sports and hobbies. Mime different activities e.g.
dancing, sewing, climbing, playing a musical instrument. Display favourite
toys and books, puzzles and games. Survey to see how much TV is watched
and what the favourite programmes are. Display any of the children's
collections of stamps, badges, coins, labels, postcards, etc. Listen to
Mozart's *Toy Symphony*.

Holes

Theme   Holes are all around us e.g. keyholes, buckets, litter bins, drains, etc. Holes can be fascinating, useful, dangerous, or holes can be home. Creatures that live underground in holes (burrows)—worms, moles, rabbits, badgers. People who work underground—miners. What gets dug out of holes in the earth—coal, iron, gold, rocks for building and precious stones. Underground railways. We have holes in our heads—mouth, nose, ear and eye. Holes can make interesting sounds—seashells, recorder, stethoscope, megaphone. How holes are made—drills, tractor diggers. Some holes shouldn't be there—holes in clothes, punctures, broken windows. Holes can be fun, but holes can be dangerous too.

Stories   The Lion who fell into a Hole p. 146
The Very Hungry Caterpillar   E. Carle (Hamish Hamilton)
Holes   P. Blakely & T. Kitada (Black)
Hans of Harlem (*Together Today* p. 184)

Poems   A mouse lived in a little hole (TLP p. 41)
A tiny, tiny worm (TLP p. 152)
If ever you should need a hole   B. Ireson (*Over & Over* p. 24)
My Father   Ted Hughes (*Meet my Folks* p. 55)
Who's in Holes?   R. Armour (World's Work)

Songs   There's a hole in my bucket (*Apusskidu* no. 16)

Prayer   68

Activities   Collect objects with holes e.g. colander, tea-strainer, sieve, net, needles, rings, straws, Swiss cheese. Print with cylinders and things with holes in. Stencil through holes e.g. doilies. Rub manhole covers. Make patterns using a hole punch, honeycomb shapes. Study the interior of a lock. Look through telescopes and kaleidoscopes.

Homes

Theme   What sort of home do you live in? Do you know your address? If you were lost could you describe where your home was? What is your house made of? What rooms do you have? What makes a house or flat into a home—the people you live with. Home is a place that you share with the people you live with. In what ways can you help to make it a happier place? As we think of the comfort of our home we should remember those people in many parts of the world who have no home.

Stories   How the Tortoise got its Shell p. 139
The Houses Built on Sand and Rock (*Matt.* 7:24)
The Three Pigs   Trad

Poems   I will build you a house (YP p. 13–27)
In the house (*This Little Puffin* p. 25–38)
This is the house that Jack built (*Puffin Nursery Rhymes* p. 23)
Hurry Home   L. Clark (HL p. 73)
Animal Houses   J. Reeves (WGMM p. 83)

Songs   We're Going Home (SSL no 58)
The wise man and the foolish man (*Okki* no. 29)
Bling Blang (S&D p. 91)

Prayers 4, 8, 17, 24, 25, 41, 52, 55

Activities   Make room models and furniture. Make rubbings from materials used in buildings e.g. bricks. Design patterns for curtains, carpets, wallpaper. Draw/collage/paint individual houses, or fantasy houses. See which building shapes have strength. Visit a building site, or special home e.g. castle. Graph the type of houses people live in. Find out about animal homes.

Hot and Cold

Theme   How do you keep warm at home and at school? What do animals do in winter to keep warm? Some hibernate in cosy nests, others grow thicker coats. What happens to these thick coats in summer? January is usually the coldest month, which is the warmest? If you are cold then running, jumping and skipping make you hotter. Using energy makes heat—that's why you get hot, then sweating helps you cool down. All things are affected by heat and cold. The amount of heat in anything is called the temperature. To measure the temperature we use a thermometer. What is the temperature today—outside and inside? This rhyme may help to remind you of average centigrade temperatures

> Five and ten and twenty-one,
> Winter, spring and summer sun'.

Stories   The Young Man and the Swallow p. 171
The Wind and the Sun   Aesop

Poem   Pease pudding hot, pease pudding cold ...   Trad.

Songs   Hot-cross buns!   Nursery rhyme
I Love the Sun (SSL no. 12)

Prayers 47, 60, 64, 65

Activities   Make a temperature graph and take daily temperature readings. Find out your body temperature. Investigate how people live in hot and cold lands. Study what happens to the body when it feels hot, and cold. Show what happens when different substances are heated e.g. wax. Study the effects of insulation—vacuum flasks and ice boxes. Show how hot air rises e.g. float a small feather over a lighted candle. Investigate the heating of a house or your school.
    (See also Ice and Snow p. 69, Sun p. 107)

Ice and Snow

Theme   When the weather is very cold and the temperature is low, then it may reach freezing point (0° Centigrade) when water turns into ice. Early morning dew turns into frost, ice forms on puddles, ponds, and even streams or rivers. Frozen rain falls as sleet, hail or snow. As water freezes it expands. This can cause pipes to burst in houses in freezing cold weather. When freezing water drips it makes icicles. Icebergs are huge lumps of ice in the sea. Refrigerators are machines which make ice, ice is used to preserve food. It is fun to skate on too, and even good to eat when it is ice-cream.

Stories   The First Snow p. 128
Good King Wenceslas p. 134
Varenka (*Together Today* p. 258)
The Snow Queen   Hans Andersen

Poems   Jack Frost   G. Setoun (YP p. 74)
Winter Morning   O. Nash (YP p. 75)
Snow   L. Clark (YP p. 76)
Snow Maidens   Norah Hussey (HL p. 72)
White fields   James Stevens (RAS p. 40)
Snowflakes   J. Lambert (SS p. 26)

Songs   See how the snowflakes are falling (SSL no. 57)
Snowflakes (*Harlequin* no. 3)
Ho! Jack Frost (*Harlequin* no. 5)
Here we go round the mulberry bush   Trad.

Prayer   60

Activities   Make long Jack Frost fingernails for nipping. Paint a picture or write a poem about Jack Frost. Make model snowmen e.g. out of toilet roll and cotton wool, with hat and scarf. Cut out snowflakes by folding and cutting paper. Act a snow play e.g. 'A Finger Play for a Snowy Day' (CFM p. 40) Study ice cubes, look at snow crystals under a microscope. Show how frozen water expands.

Movement themes—the dance of snowflakes; Watch out, Jack Frost's about! Slippery ice!

Journeys

Theme   How did you come to school today? When you travel from one place to another place it is called a journey. Most of our journeys are on foot. We must take care to have a safe journey. That means being careful on the roads and knowing the Green Cross Code. If you got lost would you know what to do? To travel safely by car we use seatbelts. We never get on or off a bus when it is moving. Never lean out of train windows. People who travel long journeys often take a map with them. A map tells you where places are and how far there is to go. Our life is rather like a journey, and we all need to help each other along the way.

Stories   St Christopher (*Together Today* p. 225)
Journeys of St Paul (*Acts* 13–18)
David's First Flight   U. Norris (TMAS p. 116)

Poems   The Airman   C. Sansom (TMAS p. 124)
The Engine Driver   C. Sansom (RAS p. 20)

Songs   The journey of life (SSL no. 28)
The train is a-coming (SSL no. 23)
Morningtown ride (SSL no. 25)
Travel on (CP no. 42)
One more step (CP no. 47)

Prayers 31, 32, 49, 50, 67

Activities   Talk about any long journeys the children have been on. Discuss how to get to distant places. Study a journey by a famous explorer. Make up a chain-story about a journey. Display pictures and pamphlets of holiday destinations at home and abroad.
(See also Transport p. 109)

Light

Theme   In winter the days are short and it gets dark early. We sometimes have to switch on the light in the daytime because the sky is dark. What makes the lights work? Before electricity was invented people had gas lights, oil lamps and candle light. What are candles made from? When the wick burns you can see the wax melting. Some lights tell you things e.g. traffic lights, belisha beacons, warning lights, neon signs. What lights can you see in the sky? Shadows—what makes them? Jesus said he was the light of the world. What is a halo?

Stories   The Man who sold his Shadow p. 150
The Wise Men and the Star (*Matt.* 2.6)
Saul sees the Light (*Acts* 9)
The Virgins and their Lamps (*Matt.* 25)
Seeing the Light (*Together Today* p. 234)

Poems   *A Riddle Rhyme*
Little Nancy Etticoat in a white petticoat
And a red nose.
The longer she stands, the shorter she grows.
(A candle)

Songs   This little light of mine (FFC p. 15)
Give me oil in my Lamp (CP no. 43)
Jesus bids us shine (MHB no. 34)
Hanukah (*Harlequin* no. 39)

Prayers 59, 70

Activities   Do wax resist drawings with candles and then paint over them with water colours. Investigate bulbs, torches and batteries. Collect pictures of the ways lights are used e.g. lighthouses, headlights, fairy lights. Study shadows, e.g. slide projector shadows, and how light is reflected from water and mirrors. Make a mobile or pictures of things that give us light.

Movement theme—pretend to be candles slowly melting and sinking. Skipping game 'Jack be nimble, Jack be quick, Jack jump over the candle-stick'.

Listen!

Theme   There are sounds all around us. Listen! What can you hear?
Some sounds that we like are called music. Sounds that we don't like we call
noises. What sounds do you like? What sounds don't you like? Some sounds
are loud, others are soft. If you listen you can hear a whisper, or even a pin
drop. People who cannot hear are deaf. People who are partially deaf can be
helped by hearing aids. Deaf people can understand what is said by lip
reading. They can even talk by using deaf and dumb sign language. Do you
know anyone who is deaf? Hearing is one of our five senses—what are the
others? How good are you at listening?

Stories   The Story of Echo   Greek myth
Jesus helps a deaf man to hear (*Mark* 7:31)

Poems   The Sounds of the Evening   E. Farjeon (FPB p. 18)
Something makes a sound (*Junior Voices I* p. 67)
Very Quiet   B. Ireson (*Over & Over Again* p. 91)
Noise   Anon (RAS p. 52)
Sounds of Spring   P. Collins (SS p. 48)

Songs   Give us Eyes (SSL no. 18)
Do your ears hang low? (*Okki* no. 25)
I listen and I listen (CP no. 60)
The music man (*Okki* no. 44)
Oh we can play on the big bass drum (*Okki* no. 45)
Old woman, old woman (*Apusskidu* no. 10)

Prayers 22, 30, 61

Activities   Experiment with sound effects e.g. clip clop of coconuts for
horses hooves; rustling dry leaves for fire; shaking a box of beads for rain.
What animal noises can you make? Make some musical instruments to play.
Tape record some sound effects for a sound quiz. Set up a sound corner
where the children can experiment. Make a telephone from plastic pots
threaded tautly with string. Listen to a shell—what is making the noise?
Investigate vibration, and rhythm. Does each child know the rhythm of his/
her name? Go on a listening walk.

Litter

Theme   When we make the world around us dirty it is called pollution. At home and school it is important to be as clean and tidy as possible. Where should rubbish be put? Litter is dirty and can be dangerous e.g. broken bottles, open tin cans, banana skins. Pollution of the atmosphere is caused by smoke, traffic and aircraft fumes, this is very bad for health especially throats and lungs. Noise pollution is caused by motor cycles, aircraft, lorries, record players, etc. Too much noise can be bad for the ears. Pollution of rivers and canals comes from industrial waste. Pollution at sea comes from oil and sewage. These can kill fish and damage sea birds. How can we help to prevent pollution?

Stories   The Tidying up of Thomas   Charlotte Hough (*Bad Boys* p. 59)

Poems   Mr Nobody   Anon (CFM p. 205)
                    The Dustbin Men   G. Harrison (*Rhyme Time* p. 54)

Songs   Milk bottle tops and paper bags (SSL no. 17)
                    The Wombling Song (*Apusskidu* no. 27)

Prayers 48, 55

Activities   Make junk models or a collage of selected waste. Design litter posters, or a new dustbin. Do a graph of the playground litter found in one week. Visit a council refuse depot to see how rubbish is sorted. Try making your own recycled paper (torn newspaper and water in a liquidiser, then press firmly to dry).

See also: *Look Around the Town* a resource pack on the urban environment which includes Teachers Notes, Frieze, Worksheets, Workcards, Flash cards, story books and glove puppets. Age range 4–7 years. From the Keep Britain Tidy Group, Bostel House, 37 West Street, Brighton BN1 2RE.

Look!

Theme   How do you see? The shape and colour of eyes. What do you like to look at? Things that we could not do if we could not see—colours, shapes, sizes, etc. A person who cannot see is blind. Blind people often have white sticks and guide dogs to help them. They can 'read' by feeling raised dots on paper—braille. Some people are blind from birth, others are blinded by accidents. The need to be careful with eyes. Things that help us see more—glasses, mirrors, telescopes, binoculars, periscopes, magnifying glasses. What we do with our eyes—blinking, winking, peeping, sleeping. The game 'I Spy with my Little Eye'. Interesting things to look at— kaleidoscopes, prisms, optical illusions, crystals, etc. Animal eyes, birds' eyes, fishes' eyes. Colour blindness. Appreciating the beauty of the physical world.

Stories   St Valentine and the Blind Girl p. 163
The Blind Man (*Mark* 8.22)
Lot's Wife (*Genesis* 13)

Poems   Horrible Things   Roy Fuller (RAS p. 54)
In the Mirror   E. Fleming (J&J p. 59)

Songs   Give to us eyes (SSL no. 18)
He gave me eyes so I could see (SSL no. 19)
Praise to God for things we see (SSL no. 20)
All things bright and beautiful (CP no. 3)

Prayers   6, 16, 22, 28, 30, 56, 65

Activities   Make a simple graph of the different colour of children's eyes in school or class. Collect things we use to help us see better— sunglasses, magnifying glass, etc. Investigate the workings of an old camera. Collect pictures of eyes, human and animal. Play looking games like I-Spy and Hunt the Thimble. Blindfold a child, see what he can recognise by feel. Close your eyes and try 'looking' with your mind's eye.

Machines

Theme   In the modern world we are surrounded by machines. What machines have you got in your house—washing machine, hoover, refrigerator, electric drill, mechanical toys, etc. What machines have you in school? There are machines for travelling in—cars, trains, bicycles, buses, boats, planes, helicopters, rockets, etc. Machines are used to make things in factories. Some machines are built like people—robots. In a way our body is a machine—it needs energy (food) to make it run, it must be cleaned and kept in good health (it needs rest and care). But there are ways in which we are different from machines—they cannot feel happy or sad, they cannot think for themselves—we can.

Stories   James and his Machines p. 141
Duggie the Digger and his Friends   M. Prescott (Puffin)

Poems   Danger: Men at Work   J. Gregory (S&D p. 92)
Steam Shovel   C. Malam (*Full Swing* p. 76)

Songs   Wheels keep turning (*Apusskidu* no. 24)
Music—Mozart's *Toy Symphony*

Prayers 32, 57

Activities   Collect pictures of machines in action, make a collage of machines. Draw or construct a robot using boxes, with tops and lids for dials, light bulbs for eyes, etc. Tape record robot messages to play inside your robot model. Display mechanical toys. Take a machine such as a clock, to pieces to see how it works. Visit a factory or machine museum.

Movement idea—Act out the moving parts of a machine in sound and movement, let each child be a working part, then put your machine together!

May Day

Theme   The first of May is May Day. It is a national holiday in Britain, and is celebrated in countries throughout the world. In the old days young people would get up early on May morning to gather branches of may-tree blossoms to decorate the house. Fairs were held in every town and village. Maypoles were set up on village greens, and everyone enjoyed a May Day holiday. A May Queen was chosen and carried round the streets with garlands of flowers and attended by maids of honour. There were maypole dances and morris dancers, which sometimes included a hobby horse. In some countries there are great parades through the streets on this day, often with marching soldiers. Which do you think is the best way of celebrating the beginning of May?

Stories   The Monster of Padstow (*Together Today* p. 208)
Robin Hood (Macdonald Starter)

Poems   We come to greet you on the first of May
And we hope you will not send us away
For we dance and sing our merry song
On our Maypole Day.

May   C. Rossetti (YP p. 61)

Songs   Nuts in May (ONS p. 11)
May Morning (*Harlequin* no. 21)
Sing a song of May-time (NCS 14)

Prayers 61, 63

Activities   Hold a May Day festival. Learn Maypole or other country dances. Make garlands of paper flowers. Choose and crown a May Queen. Make hobby horses and dress a Green Man. Hold a parade or May Fair. Cook some May Day buns. Display May blossoms.

Milk

Theme   The milk we drink comes from cows. Cows live on a dairy farm, and they produce milk to feed their calves. In the old days people used to milk their cows by hand. Today farmers have large herds of cows and the cows are milked by machine. From the farm, milk is taken by tanker to the dairy. At the dairy the milk is treated (pasteurised) and put in bottles or cartons. Milk is bought from shops or delivered by the milkman. What do we use milk for? With milk we can make other dairy products—butter, cheese, yoghurt, ice-cream, etc. Cream rises to the top of the milk. Milk is full of goodness and helps keep you strong and healthy.

Stories   The Milkmaid and her Pail p. 153
The Cow who Fell in the Canal   P. Krasilovsky and P. Spiers
(Puffin)
The Milkman   M. Harris (Dinosaur)

Poems   The Cow   R L. Stevenson (*A Child's Garden* p. 41)
Cows   J. Reeves (WGMM p. 76)
The King's Breakfast   A. A. Milne (Funny Rhymes p. 114)
Calling the Cows Home   J. Ingelow (YP p. 101)
A Herd of Little Cows (*Puffin Nursery Rhymes* p. 26)

Songs   I'd like to be a milkman (NCS 34)
Where are you going to my pretty maid? (ONS p. 25)

Prayers 15, 66

Activities   Graph or survey how many pints each family buys in one week. List all the things mum uses milk for. Draw or paint cows showing various types, colours and markings. Make models of milk floats and tankers. Show how milk goes from a cow to your own glass. Make pictures or patterns using milk bottle tops. Make your own butter, cheese or yoghurt. Collect butter, cheese and yoghurt labels—what do they tell you? Taste various cheeses. Find out what other animals give milk. Which is bigger, a pint or a litre (capacity work with bottles and containers).

The Months of the Year

Theme   There are twelve months in every year. Do the children know the names of the months? A month is a measure of time. It is roughly the time it takes for the moon to go round the earth. In the old days this time was called a *moon*th. The year is sometimes thought to be like the life of a man—the new year as a new baby, the old year as an old man, called Old Father Time. In pictures he is shown carrying a scythe and an hour glass. The months of the year were given their names by the Romans.

Stories   The Months of the Year p. 156

Poems   Thirty days hath September, April, June and November.
All the rest have thirty-one.
Except for February alone
Which has twenty-eight days clear
And twenty-nine in each leap year.

The months of the Year   Christina Rossetti (YP p. 55)
Calendar Rhyme   F. W. Watson (CFM p. 31)
Chicken Soup with Rice   Maurice Sendak (Collins)

Songs   Days of the Months (*Harlequin* no. 1)

Prayers 1, 60

Activities   How do we measure the passing of time? Display and investigate calendars and clocks. Take a clock to pieces, show how springs are made and used e.g. Jack-in-a-Box. Make a clock face with moving hands e.g. with paper plates and cardboard hands. Build a grandfather clock from box cartons. (Large numbers from old calendars are useful for making clocks, etc.) Design your own calendar. If it is Leap Year—have a leap!

Mothers

Theme   All children, like all animals, have a mother. Most children have a mother at home to love and care for them. In fact your mother was caring for you even before you were born. She was preparing a home for you and planning to take care of you even when she did not know what you looked like. When you were a baby it was probably mother who washed and dressed you and cared for you when you were hurt or afraid. Mother teaches you many things—she shows you books, she sings songs, shows you how to dress, how to keep clean and healthy. She knows how good you can be, and how naughty. Think of the ways your mother shows her love for you. How can you say thank you to mother for all she does for you? Mothering Sunday falls on the fourth Sunday in Lent, usually around 28th March.

Stories   The Monkey and her Baby p. 155
Stories of Mary the mother of Jesus.

Poems   My Mummy   B. Ireson (*Over & Over* p66)
Our Mother   Anon (CFM p. 42)

Songs   We're going home (SSL no. 59)
At half past three we go home to tea (SSL no. 58)

Prayers 25, 44, 67

Activities   Paint a picture of your mother. Make a card or small gift for Mother's Day. Display pictures showing Mary the mother of Jesus. Study how mother animals care for their young.

Number

Theme   Numbers are all around us. They are important in all our lives. Numbers help to tell us many things. They tell us how old we are, where our house or flat is in a road, what time it is, how much things cost, how to get through to someone on the telephone, where a bus is going and so on. There are numbers in every house, street and school. Numbers are fun, they help us to play many games. We need numbers to keep the score, and to make dice with. We need numbers for measuring things. There are numbers on clothes, on boxes and packets, and on machines. Some people have lucky numbers. Do you have a favourite number? Remember that numbers are there to help you, they are your friends.

Stories   The Four Fools p. 131
The Ten Commandments (*Exodus* 20)
The Twelve Apostles Chosen (*Luke* 6)
The Gift of Camels (*Together Today* p. 177)
The Wise Man of Ireland and his Cake (*Together Today* p. 267)

Poems   One Two Three (YP p. 169–181)
One, two, buckle my shoe (Nursery rhyme)
Number Songs and Rhymes (*This Little Puffin* p. 131–136)
Making Tens   M. M. Hutchinson (CFM p. 51)

Songs   God knows me (CP no. 15)
Who built the ark? (SSL no. 44)
5,4,3,2,1, and zero (SSL no. 45)
Ten in the Bed (*Apusskidu* no. 18)
The ants go marching (*Okki* no. 36)
Ten fat sausages (*Okki* no. 38)

Prayers 36, 57, 69

Activities   Sing, say and learn some number rhymes. Look for numbers all around you. Make patterns using numerals e.g. using numbers cut out of sticky paper or drawing round templates. Create a number line or number ladder—how long can you make it? Make a collage of numbered houses. Play games using numbers, e.g. hopscotch, bingo.

Our School

Theme   What is a school? A school is made up of a building and the people inside it. Do you know all the people in your school? First there are the children. These are split up into groups or classes. Then there are adults. These may be head teachers, teachers, secretary, welfare staff, kitchen staff, caretaker, cleaners, parent and student helpers. The building has a history. Do you know when it was built? It has its own shape and design, as well as its own special name. No two schools are exactly the same. Some schools overseas are very different. Schools in the past were different too. Do you think Jesus went to school?

Stories   How Jane found Friends p. 138
              Jesus in the Temple (*Luke* 2.40)
              King Alfred learns to read (*Together Today* p. 198)
              Lion at School   P. Pearce (*Stories for Five Year Olds* p. 10)

Poems   The Marrog   R. C. Scriven (*Amazing Monsters* p. 11)

Songs   This way, that a-way (*Okki* no. 10)
              Nicky, knacky, knocky, noo (*Okki* no. 42)

Prayers 8, 21, 24, 36, 41, 55, 57, 67, 69, 70

Activities   Make a big map and show the position of your school on it. Paint a frieze or collage of how your school looks on the outside, showing the play area and the games played in it. Make a model or plan of the inside of your school using boxes for rooms. Invite people from inside your school, or from other schools, to talk about their work. Use a clockface to show times of school activities. Talk about your first day at school, and discuss how to help children new to school.

Pancake Day

Theme   Shrove Tuesday is traditionally called Pancake Day. It usually falls between the end of February and the beginning of March, depending on the date of Easter. In the old days pancakes were made on this day so that all the eggs could be eaten up before Lent. Expert pancake makers can toss pancakes in the pan so that both sides are cooked. In some towns they have pancake tossing races on Pancake Day. Do you know how to make a pancake?

Stories   The Big Pancake   Trad. (Ladybird books)
The Story of the Thick, Fat Pancake   R. Bamberger (*My First Big Story Book* p. 21)
Pancakes, Pancakes!   Eric Carle (Hamish Hamilton)
The Tempting of Jesus (*Luke* 4:1–3)

Poems   Mix a pancake, stir a pancake,
Pop it in a pan.
Fry a pancake, toss a pancake,
Catch it if you can.
                    Christina Rossetti

          Pancake Day   S. Fountain (*Rhyme Time* p. 59)

Songs   Pancake Day song (*Watch* p. 38)
Shrove Tuesday (*Harlequin* no. 9)
Mix a pancake (*Harlequin* no. 10)

Prayers 52, 63

Activities   Make pancakes. Model with playdough. Set up a kitchen table with labelled utensils, implements, measures, timers. Study the weights and measure marked on boxes and packets. Discuss the need for safety rules in the kitchen.

People Who Help Us

Theme   There are many people who help us in school e.g. teachers, caretakers, dinner ladies, lollipop man or lady, visiting doctors or nurses. Many people help to look after the school building—painters, builders, engineers, carpenters. Others may help to cook school meals or tend the gardens. Parents and helpers may also help in school. Other people help us every day by bringing things to our house—postmen, milkmen, other deliveries. People help in the street—policemen, dustmen, street cleaners. People help us to travel—busmen, traindrivers, etc. Others help to serve us in shops, look after our parks, keep our zoos. Farmers and distributors help us by providing our food. Others make clothes, provide gas and electricity. In different ways we are all helping each other.

Stories   The Good Samaritan (*Luke* 10)

Poems   The Milkman   C. Sansom (YP p. 41)
The Window Cleaner   M. Long (YP p. 39)
The Dustman   C. Sansom (CFM p. 26)
The Postman   A. Horrox (S&D p. 93)
The Gas Man Cometh   M. Flanders & D. Swan (S&D p. 98)

Songs   Here we go round the mulberry bush   Trad.
The Fireman (*Apusskidu* no. 33)
Can you tell me? (*Okki* no. 55)
People who help us (*Sing, Say and Move* p. 24)

Prayers 50, 67, 69

Activities   Invite some people who help us e.g. policeman, fireman, postman to talk about their work. Mime the different jobs that people have. Graph the work that fathers and mothers do. 'When I grow up. . .' ask the children to describe the work they would like to do.

Pets

Theme   What is a pet? What pets do the children have? Having a pet means they *belong* to us. That means we must take care of them. What does taking care mean if you have a cat, dog, tortoise or rabbit? What they eat and where they live. The names we give them. The funny things they do—some things that we can't do! The things we can do that they can't. Different kinds of noises they make. Different kinds of covering—fur, shell or feathers. The way they move their tails, legs, fins or wings.

Stories   St Jerome and the Lion p. 161
St Francis and the Wolf p. 160
Greyfriars Bobby (*Together Today* p. 181)
Jacko and other Stories   J. Sutcliffe (Puffin)

Poems   The Petshop   R. Field (YP p. 117)
My Brother Bert   Ted Hughes (RAS p. 78)

Songs   The pet shop chorus (*Sing a Song* 2 no. 5)
Where and oh where has my little dog gone (*Apusskidu* no. 42)
Daddy wouldn't buy me a bow-wow (*Apusskidu* no. 43)
John Brown had a little guinea pig (*Over & Over* p. 214)

Prayers 13, 27, 54, 65

Activities   Visit a pet shop, look at the pets for sale, pet foods and accessories e.g. dog leads, budgie mirrors, mouse wheels, etc. Visit a zoo with a children's pets corner. Ask a representative from the RSPCA or PDSA to talk about looking after pets. Make pictures of pets, real and imaginary. Collect and sort magazine pictures of pets. Write about the pets you have at home, or a story of your life as a pet.

Pond Life

Theme   In the Spring ponds begin to come to life. You may see small jelly-like masses of frogs eggs floating on the surface of ponds. Do you know how they will grow? It is easy to believe in tales of frogs changing into princes as you watch frog-spawn change into tadpoles, then into frogs. Pond snails change too, from a tiny jelly-like spawn into snails. How do fish begin life? What do ponds need growing in them to keep pond life healthy? Like pond life we, too, grow and change. Ponds can be dangerous places—why?

Stories   How the Frog lost his Tail p. 137
        The Frog Prince   Grimm
        The Frog and the Ox   Aesop
        The Frogs and their King   Aesop

Poems   Daddy fell into the pond   Alfred Noyes (HL p. 61)
        Porwigles   J. Holder (FPB p. 69)
        The Tadpole   E. E. Gould (CFM p. 130)

        Hopping frog, hop here and be seen
        I'll not pelt you with stick or stone:
        Your cape is laced and your coat is green
        Goodbye, we'll let each other alone.
                         C. Rossetti

Songs   Five little frogs (*Apusskidu* no. 44)
        Frog went a-courting (*Apusskidu* no. 45)

Prayers 14, 27, 54

Activities   Draw the life-cycle of a tadpole. Study different sorts of frogs and toads. Make a collage of pond life. Investigate pond water, weed and algae. Keep some tadpoles or pond snails and observe their habits.
    Movement themes—frog hopping, snails crawling, darting dragonflies, gliding fish, etc.

Protection

Theme   We all need protection from things which might hurt us. We must help to protect others too. Our skin protects us, so do our nails and hair. Sometimes we need to protect our skin. A plaster will protect a cut knee, sun-tan oil protects the skin from sunburn. People sometimes wear rubber gloves to protect their hands. We cover some things to protect them—we cover food, put newspaper down when we are painting, etc. Some fruits and seeds are covered to protect them e.g. orange peel and conkers. So are animals e.g. hedgehogs, tortoises. A tree is protected by bark, a cactus by prickles, a knight by armour. People sometimes wear special clothes for protection—hats and suits. Car drivers and passengers need protection e.g. seatbelts. Road users need reflective clothing for protection. We are lucky to have special people to protect us—policemen, family, friends. Some people believe that God or a guardian angel protects them.

Stories   How the Tortoise got its Shell p. 139
Varenka (*Together Today* p. 258)

Poems   Hector Protector (*Colour Songs & Rhymes* p. 5, Kiddicraft)
The Hedgehog and his Coat   E. Fleming (CFM p. 156)

Songs   The Guard Song (*Apusskidu* no. 32)
When father papered the parlour (*Apusskidu* no. 34)
When a knight won his spurs (SSL no. 34)
When I needed a neighbour (SSL no. 35)

Prayers   22, 49, 50, 52, 67, 70

Activities   Make pictures of people who help us. Collect sets of shells, hats, gloves, etc. Design your own umbrella or crash helmet. Test materials to see which are waterproof. Make patterns of roof shapes. Look at your skin through a magnifying glass. What happens to unprotected food—observe mould growth.

Proverbs and Sayings

Theme   People often like to say the same thing over and over again. We call this a saying. Perhaps someone at home has a saying that they like to repeat. Some sayings have been used so often over the years that we now call them proverbs. For example 'Too many cooks spoil the broth', 'A bird in the hand is worth two in the bush', 'People who live in glass houses shouldn't throw stones', 'Look before you leap'. There is a lot that we can learn from sayings. There are many proverbs in the Bible; and the sayings of Jesus have become famous.

Stories   The Milkmaid and her Pail p. 153
The Lion's Share   Aesop
The Dog in the Manger   Aesop
How the Camel Got his Hump   Rudyard Kipling (*Just So Stories* Macmillan)

Poems   Father says   M. Rosen (FPB p. 12)
The pot calling the kettle black   P. Clarke (*Funny Rhymes* p. 88)

Songs   Jesus, friend of little children (MHB 37)
Jesus, good above all other (MHB 41)

Prayers 46, 65

Activities   Make a collection of proverbs and sayings. Draw or paint a picture to illustrate one of the sayings. Discuss the phrases you often hear said at home. Act out one of Aesop's fables which has a moral or saying attached to it. Display and discuss a poster which has a saying or slogan on it. (A catalogue of posters is available from Argus Posters, DLM House, Edinburgh Way, Harlow, Essex CM20 2HL)

Rain

Theme   There is a saying that we can expect plenty of rain if there is an R in the name of the month. All living things need water. Rainwater comes from clouds. Different kinds of rain—drizzle, showers, thunderstorms. Types of cloud, e.g. the dark nimbus clouds which bring heavy rain. Clouds make interesting shapes when blown by the wind. Have you heard the saying 'every cloud has a silver lining? And does it ever rain cats and dogs?

Stories   Jesus calms the storm (*Mark* 4:35)
Noah and the Flood (*Genesis* 6)
The day God made Rain (*I Kings* 17–18)
Timothy Puddle   H. E. Todd (*Bad Boys* p. 7)
The Rainy Morning   E. Fraser (*Tell Me a Story* p. 49)

Poems   Who Likes the Rain   Anon (CFM p. 47)
The Little Rain   Mary Coleridge (HL p. 32)
A Rainy Day   A. West (RAS p. 86)
Puddles   J. Stickells (SS p. 16)

The rain is falling all around,
It falls on field and tree,
It rains on the umbrellas here,
And on the ships at sea.
                    R. L. Stevenson

Songs   Water of Life (CP no. 2)
Morning has Broken (CP no. 1)
Little drops of Water (MHB no. 48)

Prayers 5, 9, 18, 38

Activities   Investigate plants with and without water—what effects are there? Experiment to find out what will sink and what will float in water. Make a frieze showing the story of a drop of water (the water cycle). Measure and record rainfall. Study how water is used for our daily needs, and how it is made pure for drinking. Make music with water in jars. Visit any nearby water.

Remembering (Remembrance Sunday)

Theme   Remembrance Sunday is the nearest Sunday to 11th November which is St Martin's Day. This date is when the First World War ended and it is the day each year when we remember those who died in the two World Wars. The poppy is the symbol of this day. In nearly every town and village there are war memorials built in memory of local men who died fighting for their country. Wreaths of red poppies are laid at a large memorial in London called the Cenotaph by the Queen and other leaders. Soldiers remember the poppies which grew on the battlefields of France, and make millions of poppies to be sold in the week before Remembrance Sunday, because these poppies help us to remember.

Stories   Foolish Dan p. 130
            Ewongelema (*Together Today* p. 168)

Poems   It was Long Ago   E. Farjeon (*Bits and Pieces*)
            A Memory   D. Gibson (*Times Delights* p. 20)

Songs   Father Lead me Day by Day (MHB no. 10)

Prayers 41, 44, 62, 69

Activities   Talk about what children remember about the past e.g. this time yesterday, last week, last year. What helps them to remember? Display photos, postcards, mementoes, diaries. Go and look at local memorials. What things are important to remember? Do the children know their full addresses and telephone numbers? What songs, stories and poems do they know by heart? Play memory games e.g. 'I went to market and I bought a . . .' (Name an item, next player repeats sentence adding another item and so on until someone forgets) or 'I packed my bag and I put in a . . .' Variations include starting each item with a different letter, A–Z, or choosing one letter which each item must begin with. Memory games can also involve objects on a tray which are viewed then hidden. How many objects can the children remember?

St Francis

Theme   St Francis lived many years ago in the country of Italy.
Although he was rich he gave all his money to the sick and poor, and tried to
live like Jesus. Francis wore a brown cloth robe, with a rope for a belt and no
shoes. With some friends he went round teaching and helping people. He
loved all wild creatures, animals and birds. Because he was so kind and
gentle they loved him too and came to his call. Stories are told of how he
released wild doves who had been kept in a cage, and when a fisherman
gave him a large fish he put it back in the water. St Francis is said to be the
first person who set up a crib at Christmas. Today there are monks who
dress like St Francis and spend their lives praying and helping others.

Story   St Francis and the Wolf p. 160

Poem   Praised be my Lord, for our Brother Sun,
Who caused all day his course to run.
For our Sister Moon, praised be my Lord,
By stars in heavenly hosts adored.
For our Brothers, the Wind, the Cloud, and the Air,
Whose blessings all your creatures share.
Praised be my Lord for Waters bright,
For our Brother Fire, for warmth and light,
To Mother Earth, your gifts you send,
O God our Father, and our Friend.

St Francis

Songs   All things which live below the sky (SSL no. 41)

Prayers: 63, 65

Activities   Make a frieze showing St Francis surrounded by birds and
animals. Enact one of the stories of St Francis. Invite a monk or nun to talk
about their lives. Study pictures of Assissi or stained glass windows showing
St Francis. Talk about the way children can look after animals and care for
their pets.

Saying Thank You

Theme   The last Thursday in November is called Thanksgiving Day in the U.S.A. For the American people it is a special day when they remember the first harvest festival held by the pilgrim fathers at New Plymouth in New England in 1621. At this first harvest festival roast turkeys were eaten because they were plentiful in New England. Today American families still have roast turkey on this day.

It is a good idea from time to time to count your blessings and be thankful for the good things of life. What are you thankful for in your life? If someone does something special for us, or gives something to us, we should remember to say thank you.

Stories   The Man who said Thank You p. 149

Poems   Little deeds of kindness
Little words of love,
Make this earth an Eden
Like the heaven above.
                Isaac Watts

Songs   Thank you (FFC p. 3)
Stand up, clap hands, shout thank you Lord (SSL no. 14)
Think of a world without any flowers (SSL no. 15)
Thank you Lord (CP no. 32)
Now thank we all our God (CP no. 38)
Oh thank the Lord (MHB no. 16)

Prayers 2, 33, 38, 39, 52, 53, 54, 61, 66, 67, 68

Activities   Find out more about the Pilgrim Fathers and their ship the *Mayflower*. Talk about or make a list of the blessings in your life. Write a thank you letter to someone who has helped or given something to you. Find out how to say thank you in different languages.

The Sea

Theme   Most of the world is covered by the sea. How many children
have seen the sea? What colour is it? The sea sometimes looks blue on a
sunny day, or grey when the sky is overcast. The colour of the sea reflects
the sky. If the water is deep it usually looks green, but if you scoop water out
of the sea it is colourless like tapwater. The sea is full of life, plants and
animals—some large, others so small you cannot see them. What taste does
the sea have? Why? What people work at sea? Why can the sea be so
dangerous?

Stories   Jonah and the Whale (*Jonah* 1)
Jesus sleeps in a boat (*Mark* 4:35–41)
Jesus meets the fishermen (*Matt.* 18. 22)
Jesus calms the storm (*Mark* 4)
Bertha gets into trouble—L. Smith (*More Stories to Tell* p. 95)

Poems   Storm-wind   C. Rossetti (HL p. 27)
Until I saw the sea   L. Moore (YP p. 67)
The Jumblies   Edward Lear
The Owl and the Pussy Cat   Edward Lear

Songs   When lamps are lighted in the town (SSL no. 26)
Now Jesus one day (SSL no. 30)
Apusski dusky (*Apusskidu* no. 51)
Bobbing up and down like this (*Okki* no. 7)
Sea Songs (*Sing a Song 2*: 99–105)

Prayers 9, 37, 45, 49

Activities   Listen to the sounds of the sea—in a shell, or other sound
effects. Make a fishing game with a magnet and cardboard fish with metal
fasteners. Make an underwater montage and/or a fish mobile. Play 'fish the
kipper' with paper fish shapes. Make different ship models out of junk
materials. Origami—make a paper boat.

Seeds

Theme   All flowering plants grow from a seed. There are different kinds of seeds—large and small, seeds that fly, seeds that we can eat. What does a seed need to grow?—water, light and warmth, and food (a seed has food stored inside it from the leaves and the soil). A large tree can grow from a small seed, a dull seed can produce a beautiful flower. Plants die but their seeds make new plants. Look out for flowers and trees shedding their leaves in autumn. Not every seed comes up—there is an old rhyme about planting, 'One for the mouse, one for the crow, one to rot, one to grow'. It is often best to grow seeds indoors first. What seeds that you eat could you plant?

Stories   The Enormous Turnip   Trad. (Ladybird Books, etc.)
Jack and the Beanstalk   Trad. (Ladybird Books, etc.)
The Sower (*Matt.* 13, *Luke* 8)
Johnny Appleseed (*Together Today* p. 194)

Poems   Little Brown Seed   R. Bennett (CFM p. 58)
A Growing Rhyme   J. M. Westrup (CFM p. 64)
The Magic Seeds   J. Reeves (WGMM p. 148)
Seeds   W. de la Mare (S&D p. 30)
The Seed   A. Fisher (S&D p. 31)
Seeds   H.I. Rostron (S&D p. 45)

Songs   The Farmer comes to scatter the seed (SSL no. 56)
We plough the fields and scatter (NCS 93)

Prayers 27, 60

Activities   Grow beans on blotting paper. Collect seeds and study seed sizes e.g. coconut, corn, walnut, dandelion, bean, apple, cherry, melon, conker, acorn, etc. Study the different shapes of seeds (using a magnifying glass). Display large pictures of plants with the real seeds from which they grow. Look for seeds in a wood, hedgerow or meadow (e.g. grass seeds) and show how seeds can be taken from dead flowers or plants. Sort a seed collection into sets.

Sheep

Theme   Wool comes from sheep. Sheep are kept in flocks on farms.
Who looks after sheep? Sheep usually have their lambs in spring. What are
mother and father sheep called? (Ewes and rams). Farmers go to special
markets to buy and sell sheep. Sheep are dipped to keep their coats healthy.
In the winter their coats grow thick to keep them warm. When spring comes
the sheep are sheared. A sheep's woolly coat is called a fleece. Wool is spun
on a spinning wheel or a machine at a mill. Wool is treated and dyed, then it
is ready for knitting and weaving. What things are made from wool?

Stories   The Lost Sheep p. 147
The Boy who Cried Wolf   Aesop
Sarah the Lamb   V. M. Colwell (*Tell Me a Story* p. 150)

Poems   Mary had a little lamb (Nursery Rhyme)
The Wolf and the Lambs   I. O. Eastwick (CFM p. 43)
Mrs Grip was always knitting   C. Culshaw (*Read Me a Story*
p. 89)

Songs   The Lord's my Shepherd (CP no. 56)
Baa, baa black sheep (ONS p. 3)
Little Boy Blue (ONS p. 15)
Little Bo-Peep (ONS p. 33)

Prayers 18, 27, 54

Activities   Collage with wool a flock of sheep. Try to find some sheep's
wool, pull out the fibres and roll it in the hands. Try making simple
vegetable dyes for wool. Examine odd lengths of knitting wool under a
magnifying glass. Try simple weaving with wools. Make woollen dolls.
Study different plys of wool, long and short fibres, etc.

Shopping

Theme   The New Year is always a time for sales in shops. Why is this? Everyone has to go shopping, some people prefer big shops and supermarkets, others prefer small shops, and some go to open air markets. Shops sell different things. Where would you go to buy stamps? (Talk about the post office) Where would you buy bread? In a market you buy things from stalls. Where is your local shopping centre? There are different ways of paying for goods—using cash, cheque or bank-card. What would you do if you bought something that went wrong? In big shops they have store detectives. What do you think their job is?

Stories   The Old Woman and the Pig (Ladybird)
Tassletip Buys a Present (Ladybird)
The Five Pound Note (*Together Today* p. 172)

Poems   An Old Rhyme (CFM p. 14)
At the Supermarket   B. Ireson (*Rhyme Time* p. 164)
General Store   R. Field (YP p. 125)
Off we go to market   G. A. Smith (CFM p. 48)
Old Mother Hubbard   Nursery rhyme

Songs   Come let us remember the joys of the town (SSL no. 7)
Tall shop in the town (TLP p. 66)

Prayers 66, 67

Activities   Make a classroom shop, price the goods and practise buying and selling. Visit local shops or a market. Make coin rubbings, design new coins and notes for the class shop. Sort magazine pictures matching articles to shops. Make up shopping lists from mail order catalogues. Set up a class post office, design stamps for school use.

Signs and Symbols

Theme   There is a lot that we can tell each other without using words. We can say things using our hands e.g. pointing, shaking fist in anger, shaking hands to show friendship and greeting, stop!, and come on, etc. Policemen and cyclists use hand signals. There are many signs in the street—school sign, drivers L plate, traffic signals, symbols on toilet doors. We can recognise things without words e.g. flags, badges, rosettes, barbers pole, pub signs. Signs are sometimes used when words would not be heard—lighthouse lights, signalling aircraft landing, traffic indicators. Signs are used in music and maths when words would take up too much space. Signs are often used in road maps and weather maps. The Christian sign is a cross—why is that sign used?

Stories   The Hungry Lion and the Wise Fox   Aesop
The Secret Birthday Message   E. Carle (Hamish Hamilton)
Robinson Crusoe and the Footprint (*Together Today* p. 169)

Poem   Red sky at night
Shepherd's delight
Red sky in the morning
Shepherd's warning.

Songs   Songs in which actions can be used in place of words.

Prayer 50

Activities   Make up a story using picture symbols for words at intervals. Study road signs, have a walk to look at local signs and symbols. Paint some flags, pub signs, school badge. Make a model of a lighthouse (e.g. using cardboard tube container, bulb and battery) Study animal tracks. Talk about the signs of the zodiac.

Sleep

Theme   Many animals and insects go to sleep through the cold days of winter. What animals are they? This kind of sleep is called hibernation. Would you like to go to sleep in autumn and wake up in the spring? The need for sleep to rest our body, especially for growing bodies. What happens during sleep? Dreams and nightmares. How do you feel in the morning if you go to bed late? Some people find it difficult to sleep, what helps you to go to sleep—counting sheep? People sleep in different positions, on different kinds of beds, at different times (e.g. night workers) wearing different nightclothes. But they all need the right amount of sleep. Everything in nature needs a rest.

Stories   Why the Bat flies at Night p. 168
Jacob's Ladder (*Genesis* 28)
Rip van Winkle (*Together Today* p. 222)
Sleeping Beauty   Trad.

Poems   Wee Willie Winkie   Nursery rhyme
Cats Sleep Anywhere   E. Farjeon (FPB p. 58)
Ned   E. Farjeon (YV p. 67)
Before Sleeping   Anon (*Times Delights* p. 84)

Songs   Father, we thank you for the night (SSL no. 1)
Ten in the bed (*Apusskidu* no. 18)
Bananas in pyjamas (*Apusskidu* no. 20)
Give me joy in my heart (MHB no. 17)
Strangest Dream (FFC p. 26)
Frère Jacques (ONS p. 31)

Prayers 1, 21, 51

Activities   Find out how many hours of sleep the children have. Discuss, or chart, the different bedtimes. Make pictures of your dreams or nightmares. Sing lullabies and see how many different lullabies the children know.

Small Creatures

Theme   Some of the most interesting creatures in the world are the smallest. Small creatures can live almost anywhere—in houses, under stones, in small holes, underneath leaves. Most small creatures are insects. What might you find under a stone? Woodlice, centipedes, caterpillars, snails, ladybirds, etc. Have you ever found a spider? Under the earth you might find worms. Ants live together in a nest—you can get black ants, red ants, wood ants, etc. Ants collect honeydew from aphids (greenfly). Small creatures can damage plants—slugs, blackfly, greenfly, whitefly, locusts, caterpillars. Stick insects are fascinating creatures—what do they look like? Insects are important food for birds.

Stories   The Ant and the Grasshopper p. 119
The Bad-tempered ladybird   E. Carle (Hamish Hamilton)
Anansi the Spider (*Together Today* p. 138)

Poems   Creatures Small (a section of poems in *Fancy Free*)
Tell me little woodworm   S. Milligan (*Silly Verse* p. 31)
The Centipede   E. Craster (RAS p. 82)
Snail   J. Tomkins (RAS p. 58)
Slugs   J. Kitching (FPB p. 73)

Songs   I Love God's Tiny Creatures (SSL no. 42)
The Ants go Marching (*Okki* no. 36)
All things which live below the sky (SSL no. 41)

Prayers 13, 14, 54, 65

Activities   Make models or collage pictures of small creatures. Show symmetry by cut-outs or blot prints e.g. butterflies. Keep some small creatures for studying at close hand. Snail shell pattern—spiral work. Show life-cycle of an insect in strip cartoon or frieze. Sort into sets the insects with similar characteristics—wings, number of legs, etc. Go on a small creature safari, turn over some stones and record what you see. Find out which small creatures are helpful and which harmful to man.
    Music and movement—hopping, wriggling, sliding, etc.

Spiders

Theme   One of the loveliest sights of Autumn is a perfect spider's web hung with dew, glistening in the morning sun. Have the children noticed any spiders' webs recently? Spiders are useful because they help to keep down a number of insects that are pests—what insects are they? Spiders are hardworking, it takes a long time for them to spin a web. Some tropical spiders dig holes in the ground, they are called trapdoor spiders—why? Spiders are not insects—what is special about them?

Stories   Why the Spider lives in a Web p. 170
Robert the Bruce and the Spider (*Together Today* p. 223)
The Story of Arachne   Greek legend
The Anansi Stories

Poems   Little Miss Muffet   Nursery rhyme
Good Company   Leonard Clark (*Collected Poems*)
No Jewel   W. de la Mare (*Fancy Free* p. 98)

Songs   I know an old lady who swallowed a fly (*Over and Over* p. 186)
The Spider and the Fly (ONS p. 26)

Prayers 14, 65

Activities   Make spider models e.g. out of the cup sections of pulp eggboxes pierced with four pipe cleaners—painted and decorated. Draw spiders webs, or make them with black thread. Learn about spirals. Find pictures and books about real spiders—make a display. Look out for spiders' egg sacs (keep them to see if they hatch out!)
     Movement theme—show a spider catching a fly in dramatic mime.

Sports

Theme   Sports are games which are usually played outside. Schools often hold Sports Day in the summer. In a race the first person past the finishing line is the winner, the next person is second, the next is third and so on. There are many kinds of races—running, egg-and-spoon, sack, etc. There are different sports at different times of the year—winter sports like skiing and football, and summer sports like cricket and tennis. Some sports involve animals, like horse racing. Water sports include swimming, rowing and ice-skating. Sport helps to keep you fit and healthy. Many people like to watch sports—what sports do people watch or play in your family? A good sport is someone who does not mind losing. Are you a good sport?

Stories   The Fox and the Crab p. 132
The Hare and the Tortoise   Aesop

Poem   A rabbit raced a turtle (*Funny Rhymes* p. 92)

Songs   For all the strength we have (SSL no. 16)
Hands to work and feet to run (SSL no. 21)
The no-laugh race (*Okki* no. 52)
In our work and in our play (MHB no. 46)

Prayers 20, 24, 53

Activities   Hold a sports day. Visit a local sports ground, watch training or a sport being played. Display pictures, photos and equipment used in sport. Make friezes of winter and summer sports.
Movement—mime sportsmen and sportswomen in action. Practice the exercises used in training.

Spring

Theme   What are the signs of spring? In parks and gardens seeds are being planted and green plants are pushing through the earth. Birds are busy building nests and laying eggs. Migrant birds return. On trees buds and blossom appear. For some animals it is the end of hibernation. On farms it is the time for sowing and the birth of young animals. The weather becomes warmer, the days longer. In homes it is often the time for spring cleaning and preparation for the summer as winter clothes are put away. Spring is a time for new life and new beginnings.

Stories   The Young Man and the Swallow p. 171
The Parable of the Sower (*Matt.* 13)
The Tortoise's Picnic   Anon (*More stories to tell* p. 88)

Poems   Spring   R. Wilson (YP p. 60)
Spring Song   W. Blake (*Fancy Free* p. 44)

Spring is showery, flowery, bowery,
Summer hoppy, croppy, poppy,
Autumn is wheezy, sneezy, freezy,
Winter slippy, drippy, nippy.

Songs   Who can see the great wind blow? (SSL no. 52)
Spirit of God (CP no. 89)
All the flowers are waking (SSL no. 48)
Snowdrop bells (*Harlequin* no. 11)
It happens each spring (*Harlequin* no. 15)

Prayers 5, 27, 61, 65

Activities   Make a spring frieze or collage. Display spring flowers. Place twigs with buds on them in jars of water to see how they grow e.g. horse chestnut, catkins, forsythia. Show a birds nest. Set up a display of spring books in the book corner.

Movement themes—the growth of flowers, birth and play of young animals, spring cleaning.

Stars

Theme   When night comes, stars begin to shine in the sky. They are there in the sky all the time but we only see them at night. There is only one star we can see in the daytime—the sun. The sun is a star, nearest to us of all the stars. Stars are balls of fire like our sun, they look small because they are a long way away. At night we can see about 2000 stars. But with a small telescope we can see about 10,000 stars. There are many more than this, more than anyone can count. A long time ago people saw pictures in the stars, pictures of animals and gods. Sometimes starry lights shoot across the sky. Have you ever seen a shooting star?

Stories   The Girl who liked watching Stars p. 133
The Dolphin and the Lyre (*Together Today* p. 164)
The Star of Bethlehem (*Matt.* 2)

Poems   All day long the sun shines bright,
Then moon and stars come out at night,
From twilight time they fill the skies,
And watch the world with quiet eyes.

The Falling Star   S. Teasdale (*Rhyme Time* p. 62)

Songs   Can you count the stars (SSL no. 25)
Twinkle, twinkle, little star (SSL no. 46)
God who put the stars in space (SSL no. 47)

Prayer 51

Activities   Make a mobile of stars. Stick star shapes in patterns on dark paper. Look through a telescope and display pictures of large telescopes. Find out which direction the North or Pole Star should be. Paint or show a starfish. Study the flag of the USA, or other star flags.
Movement—make star shapes.

Stones

Theme   Stones are part of the treasure of the earth. Some stones are ordinary, some are beautiful, and some are precious. Precious stones are called jewels. Do the children know the names and colours of any jewels? Stones are useful too—e.g. stepping stone, milestone, millstones, stone fountains, tombstones. Building—slate is a roofing stone, sandstone and granite are used for walls, marble for more decorative building. Gravel for roads, pebbles for paths. Some old streets are cobbled. Stones have interesting shapes and colours. Cavemen used flintstones as tools and weapons. Why are stones at the seaside so smooth? If you have a polishing kit you can polish your own stones. A geologist studies stones.

Stories   The Crow and the Jug   Aesop p. 123
The Rich Man's Diamond p. 159
David's stone kills Goliath (*I Samuel* 17)

Poems   An emerald is as green as grass
A ruby as red as blood
A sapphire shines as blue as heaven,
A flint lies in the mud.
A diamond is a brilliant stone,
To catch the world's desire,
An opal holds a fiery spark,
But a flint holds fire.
                    Christina Rossetti

The Black Pebble   James Reeves (RAS p. 49)
Pebbles   Edith King (CFM p. 114)

Songs   Daisies are our Silver (MHB no. 63)
The Building Song (CP no. 61)

Prayer   68

Activities   Collect different sorts of stones to look at and feel. Use large smooth stones from the beach to paint and varnish. Make sculptures from smooth pebbles using a strong glue e.g a stone with a tail for a mouse, one large with five small ones for a tortoise. If you have no tumble polishing kit varnish your special stones. Look at interesting ways stone is used in your locality. Study fossils. Make the Crown Jewels out of plastic shapes, coloured Cellophane, gold paper and silver foil. Display and study reference books on rocks and minerals. Find out about Stonehenge.

Strength

Theme   We are surrounded by strong things—the buildings we live in, furniture, machines, etc. What are the strongest materials—wood, metal, plastic? Plants need to be strong too, to withstand rain and wind. Many animals are very strong—which do you think are the strongest animals? Our bodies are growing stronger as we grow up—what gives us strength? Good food and exercise. Where strength comes from—our muscles. The people that need to be very strong—athletes, gymnasts, builders, wrestlers, etc. Strength of character—being strong inside and standing up for what is right.

Stories   David and Goliath (*I Samuel* 17)
Samson (*Judges* 13)
St Christopher (*Together Today* p. 225)
The Story of Atlas   Greek legend
Stories of Giants

Poem   Samson Fullength   H. Hancock (SS p. 58)

Song   For all the strength we have (SSL no. 16)

Prayers 18, 19, 66

Activities   Test to see how strong the children are by pulling a spring balance or pressing on a compression scale. Study the work and position of muscles. Flex some muscles—try smiling! Paint or draw a picture of a strong person or giant.

Movement themes—strong shapes and gestures, lifting weights, strong animals. Act out the story of someone who used his strength for good.

Summer Holidays—At the Seaside

Theme   Summer is a time for holidays. What is a holiday? Originally holidays were holy days, Where are you going for your holidays? Probably either to the country or the seaside. Some people go abroad others stay at home. There are lots of interesting things to do at the seaside. If it is sandy you can make sandcastles or draw pictures in the sand. When the tide comes in sandcastles are often washed away. We can never be sure how safe the sea will be. If the waves are rough or the water is deep the sea can be a dangerous place. If there are rock pools it is fun to explore them and look for sea creatures. Some people like beachcombing—hunting for shells and interesting stones. There are seagulls, fishing boats and a lot more beyond the far horizon.

Stories   Mary and her Bones p. 151
The Story Jesus told by the Seaside (*Mark* 4.1)
Jesus has breakfast by the Sea (*John* 21:4–14)
The Story of King Canute   Trad.

Poems   At the Seaside   R. L. Stevenson (HL p. 23)
Four Little Girls   A. E. Dudley (HL p. 64)
There are big waves   E. Farjeon (WGMM p. 114)

Songs   What fun it is beside the sea (NCS 75)
Take me to the Seaside (*Harlequin* no. 27)

Prayers   15, 31, 53

Activities   Display the treasures children have found at the seaside, shells, seaweed, driftwood, together with reference books to help identification. Make a collage or painting of seaside activities. Label a shell chart, construct shell pots and plaques. Sort shells into sets. Paint pebbles to make paperweights. Thread shell necklaces. Study fossils. Tongue twister—'She sells sea shells ...' Make a summer scrapbook.
   Movement theme—waves and sea creatures.

Summer Holidays—In the Country

Theme   If you visit the country you should remember the Countryside Code. Remember to keep to paths across farmland, close farm gates, leave no litter, never damage fences, hedges and walls, guard against all risk of fire, keep dogs under proper control. Beware of dangers in the country— getting too near the banks of rivers, streams or canals, eating strange fruits or berries, getting lost, etc. Things to see and enjoy in the country—farms, fields, woods, hills and mountains. Going on a nature ramble, what to take with you, what you might find.

Stories   The Town Mouse and the Country Mouse p. 167
              Pyp goes to the Country   V. Colwell (TMAS p. 96)

Poems   The Farmyard   A. A. Attwood (CFM p. 57)
              The Farm—section of poems in *This Little Puffin* p. 75–86

Songs   We plough the fields and scatter (NCS 93)
              I went to visit a farm one day (*Sing a Song* I no. 7)
              Old Macdonald had a Farm   Trad.

Prayers 31, 45, 53, 61, 65

Activities   Make a model farm on cardboard or wood with animals, corn store, farmhouse, fields of crops, etc. Make models of tractors and machinery. Hold a picnic out of doors e.g. a teddy bears picnic. Go on a nature trail or ramble, display and record what you saw. Collect postcards and pictures of country places. Illustrate a poster or picture on the theme of taking care of the countryside.

Sun

Theme   The sun is a good friend to us. Without the sun there would be no warmth or light, in fact no life at all. Long ago people worshipped the sun as a god. We now know that the sun is a star, just like the other stars you see in the night sky. The sun is our own star, much closer to us than any of the others. The sun is a round ball, a sphere. It has a family of planets which go around it. Our earth is one of these nine planets, it spins round once a day, so we face the sun in daytime, and see no sunlight at night. It takes the earth one year to travel round the sun. The sun is a long way away, if you could drive a car there it would take you over 200 years to reach the sun.

Stories   The Man who sold his Shadow p. 150
                The Day the Sun stood still (*Joshua* 10)
                The Wind and the Sun   Aesop
                The Story of Phaethon (*Watch* p. 20)
                Why Summer Days are Longer (*Together Today* p. 263)

Poems   The Sun   A. Fisher (WGMM p. 96)
              The Sun   J. Edwards (WGMM p. 97)
              The Sun   P. Clarke (B&P)
              Sunning   J. S. Tippett (YP p. 107)
              My Shadow   R. L. Stevenson (*A Child's Garden* p. 35)

Songs   I have seen the golden sunshine (SSL no. 6)
              I love the sun (SSL no. 12)
              We praise you for the sun (SSL no. 13)
              The Sun has got his Hat on (*Watch* p. 16)

Prayers 5, 40, 53, 65

Activities   Make pictures of the sun and the planets. Build a model Stonehenge. Find out about eclipses—the next one in Britain will be 11th August, 1999. How old will you be then? Make a sundial. Discuss why it is dangerous to stare directly at the sun.

   Movement—do a sun worship dance, move in circles and revolve slowly like planets.

Teeth

Theme   Teeth are our friends, but they need looking after. We are born without any teeth but they soon begin to grow. We have twenty first teeth, later they become loose and fall out. New teeth grow where the first ones were. These second teeth have to last for ever so we must take care of them. An older child has thirty-two permanent teeth. It is important to brush your teeth regularly. Eating an apple or carrot can help to clean your teeth. Some foods are good for teeth, like milk, eggs and cheese. Some foods can harm our teeth—sweets, sticky cakes, sugary drinks. They can make our teeth ache. A dentist helps you to care for your teeth. Animals have different kinds of teeth depending on what they eat, meat eaters have sharp pointed teeth, those that eat grass and leaves have flat teeth for chewing. You have both kinds.

Stories   The Lion and the Mouse   Aesop
The Wigglish Tooth   H. Creswell (*Bad Boys* p. 95)
Topsy and Tim visit the dentist   J. & G. Adamson (Blackie)
Emma goes to the Dentist   G. Wolde (Brockhampton)

Poems   Rosemary's Teeth   M. Dugan (FPB p. 101)
Night Starvation   C. Blyton (*Rhyme Time* p. 102)

Through the teeth, past the gums,
Look out stomach, here it comes!

Song   My Teeth (*Sing, Say and Move* p. 13)

Prayer   66

Activities   Make a collage of smiles from magazine pictures. Design posters for care of teeth. Collect and draw teeth and animal skulls. Survey or graph how often children clean teeth, favourite toothpaste, number of teeth. Make pictures or collect wrappings of sets of food good and bad for teeth. Invite a dentist to talk about his/her work. Look at a set of false teeth.
    Information: Health Education Council, 78 New Oxford Street, WC1A 1AH. General Dental Council, 37 Wimpole Street, London W1

Transport

Theme   The development of transport began with the invention of the wheel. Wheels go round. What shape are wheels? Where can you see wheels—cars, bicycles, prams, wheelbarrows. Wheels in machines—cogwheels in clocks, tape recorder wheels. Cartwheels. Reasons for transport—pioneers, explorers and inventors. Present day transport—sea, land and air. Wheels in the home—washing machine/spin dryer, can opener. Transport in the street, at the farm, in sports. Transport of the future.

Stories   Duggie the Digger and his Friends   M. Prescott (Puffin)
Huff and Puff   B. K. Wilson (*Time for a Story* p. 11)
The Little Car has a Day Out   L. Berg (Pan)
The Bus that Wouldn't Go   M. Law (*Time for a Story* p. 88)

Poems   *This Little Puffin* p. 71–74
The Song of the Engine   H. Worsley-Benison (RAS p. 46)
Motor Cars   R. B. Bennett (S&D p. 87)

Songs   Wheels keep turning (*Apusskidu* no. 24)
The train is a-coming (*Apusskidu* no. 23)
She'll be coming round the mountain (*Apusskidu* no. 26)
The wheels on the bus (*Okki* no. 32)
Riding in my car (S&D p. 87)

Prayers 32, 49

Activities   Make circle patterns of wheels. Collect and measure wheels. Investigate a bicycle wheel—spokes, chains, tyres. Survey all the wheels in the school. Create models or a frieze of different forms of transport. Make a tank from cotton reels, elastic bands and matches. Make different tyre rubbings.

(See also Journeys p. 70)

Trees

Theme   What is a tree? A tree is a plant which needs light, air, water, soil and sun. Trees grow from seeds—acorn into oak! Parts of a tree—roots, trunk, branches, twigs, leaves, bark, etc. A tree through the year, seasonal changes, evergreen and deciduous trees. Shape of leaves, colour and texture. Fruit from trees. Creatures that live in trees. Shade and shelter. Things made from wood in the school, at home, in gardens, on the sea, etc. Different kinds of wood. How trees are made into paper—the need for conservation. Telling the age of a tree.

Stories   The Story of Zacchaeus (*Luke* 19)
Palm Sunday (*Matt* 21, *Mark* 11 or *John* 12)
Johnny Appleseed (*Together Today* p. 194)
The Fir Tree and the Bramble   Aesop
The Trees and the Axe   Aesop

Poems   Trees   H. Behn (WGMM p. 107)
Trees   S. Coleridge (CFM p. 96)
The Tree on the Hill (HL p. 65)
Finders-Keepers   Cicely Barnes (HL p. 74)
In the Wood (*This Little Puffin* p. 89–96)

Songs   Somebody Greater (CP no. 5)
Who's that sitting in the sycamore tree? (SSL no. 32)
The Tree in the Wood (S&D p. 44)
Neath the spreading chestnut tree (*Okki* no. 23)
I had a little nut tree   Nursery rhyme

Prayers 5, 27, 38, 61

Activities   Visit a wood, forest or common to collect leaves, bark, seeds and to look at tree shapes. Visit a timber yard, carpenter's shop or furniture factory. Invite a carpenter to talk about his tools and what he makes. Make a frieze showing a tree in each season. Make patterns of leaf prints and bark rubbings. Collect pictures or objects of wood. Make boats, planes, masks, etc. from softwood offcuts. Plant some tree seeds—grow a forest!

Valentines

Theme   On 14th February we celebrate St Valentine's day by sending Valentine cards to those we love. St Valentine was a priest who lived in Rome. He was killed in the year AD 270 for giving shelter to Christians. At this time of year there was a Roman festival of love when young people chose their sweethearts by drawing lots. As Valentine died at this time he became associated with the feast of love. On this day birds are supposed to choose their mates and start to build their nests. Perhaps that is why you often see lovebirds as decorations on Valentine cards. Often you do not know who a Valentine card was sent from. One old superstition says that your true love is the first boy (or girl) you see on Valentine's day.

Stories   St Valentine and the Blind Girl p. 163
St Valentine and the Birds (*Together Today* p. 230)
Be My Valentine   M. Cohen (World's Work)

Poem   Roses are Red
Violets are blue
Carnations are sweet
And so are you.

Song   Valentine Questions (*Harlequin* no. 7)

Prayers 20, 25, 39, 48, 63

Activities   Make a Valentine card e.g. cut large heart shapes and decorate with pictures from magazines, doily paper, lace, sequins, etc. Write a Valentine verse or message inside the card. Make posies e.g. roses, violets and carnations out of tissue paper, to give to your true love.

Who's Afraid?

Theme   We are all afraid of something. Different people are afraid of different things. Some people are afraid of the dark. People are often afraid of what they cannot see. Fear is a good thing if it makes you careful. People are usually more frightened if they are alone. Have you ever been afraid of strange sounds or shadows in the night. Some people are frightened of animals e.g. dogs, spiders or snakes. Thunderstorms make some people scared. Others are frightened going to the dentist. People who are scared sometimes bite their fingernails, their teeth may chatter, their knees knock or even the hair stand on end. What are you scared of?

Stories   The Timid Hares p. 166
David and Goliath (*I Samuel* 17)
Where the Wild Things Are   Maurice Sendak (Bodley Head)
The Owl who was Afraid of the Dark   Jill Tomlinson (Puffin)

Poems   It's dark outside (PPB p. 17)
In the Dark   J. Pridmore (FPB p. 21)
The Silent Spinney   S. Redmond (FPB p. 114)
Adventures of Isabel   Ogden Nash (YV p. 72)
I'm not frightened of pussy cats   Spike Milligan (RAS p. 9)

Songs   Who's Afraid of the Big Bad Wolf?
I whistle a happy tune (*Apusskidu* no. 3)
When a knight won his spurs (CP no. 50)
All alone (*Over and Over* p. 88)

Prayers 18, 21, 22, 42, 49, 50

Activities   Talk about the things that scare you, and find out who else feels the same. Paint or draw what frightens you most e.g. monsters, ghosts, spiders.
Movement themes—in the dark, creeping on tiptoe, acting scared.

Refer also to: What are you scared of?   H. Larsen (Black)

Wind

Theme   'As the days grow longer, The winds grow stronger' is an old country saying. Air is all around us, we cannot see it but it is there all the same. There is a layer of air over the whole earth. We all need air to breathe, without air we could only live for a few minutes. When the air moves we call it a wind. Light winds are called breezes. Strong winds are called storms and gales. There is a lot of power in wind. Wind helps yachts to sail, windmills to turn, kites and gliders to fly. A weather vane can tell you which way the wind is blowing. Wind helps to scatter seeds and to dry washing. How can you tell if it is a windy day?

Stories   The Wind and the Sun (*Together Today* p. 265)
The Little Storm   R. Neumann (*More Stories to Tell* p. 78)
The Wind that Wanted its own Way   A. Hamilton (*Bad Boys* p. 41)
The Wind in the Wood   Lord Dunsany (RMAS p. 26)

Poems   White Sheep   W. H. Davies (HL p. 13)
Storm-wind   C. Rossetti (HL p. 27)
The Wind   J. Reeves (RAS p. 73)
The Night Wind   C. Morin (RAS p. 55)

Songs   Who can see the great wind blow? (SSL no. 52)
Michael Finnigan (*Apusskidu* no. 22)
The wind blow east (*Apusskidu* no. 30)
The north wind (*Harlequin* no. 6)

Prayer 65

Activities   Make a paper windmill. Set up a wind vane—study the direction of the wind. Draw a weather vane e.g. a cock, or your own design. Find out where North, South, East and West are. Look at a compass. Make or borrow an anemometer to see how fast the wind blows. Go to an open space to fly a kite. Design or make kites. Study the work of windmills. Set up wind chimes.

Winter

Theme   Winter is the time when much of nature goes to sleep. All living things have had a busy time during the summer, and must rest ready for new growth when the spring comes. Many animals hibernate under the earth. Some plants seem to hibernate almost like animals. Plants which have bulbs store up food for the winter and, like the dormouse, grow fat before resting. We have to heat our houses and put on winter clothes. Fog and ice can cause accidents on the roads. Many animals, especially birds, find it difficult to get enough food.

Stories   The Ant and the Grasshopper p. 119
How Winter came to earth (*Together Today* p. 190)

Poems   Winter Morning   Ogden Nash (RAS p. 59)
Jack Frost in the Garden   J. P. Smelton (CFM p. 88)

The North wind doth blow, and we shall have snow,
    And what will the robin do then, poor thing?
He'll sit in a barn, and keep himself warm,
    And hide his head under his wing, poor thing.

Songs   Little birds in winter time (SSL no. 43)
Ho! Jack Frost (*Harlequin* no. 5)
In the winter birds need food (NCS 26)

Prayer   60

Activities   Make a winter frieze or collage. Collect winter words. Study and draw animal tracks—how many footprints can you recognise? Display and identify examples of evergreen plants. Set up a simple bird table with suitable food and a dish of water. (See also Ice and Snow p. 69)

Working Together

Theme   There is a saying 'Many hands make light work'. We should always be ready to give a hand to help other people. What do you do to help at home? The jobs around the house that need doing. Being helpful to other members of the family. Helping at school—teachers, friends, cleaners. Can you think of ways you can be helpful to teachers and friends? All around the world there are people in need of help—those hit by disasters, the old, children who are hungry, handicapped, or orphans. There is no problem that we cannot overcome if we work together and help each other.

Stories   The Parts of the Body p. 158
The Bundle of Sticks p. 121
Jesus chooses Twelve Apostles (*Luke* 6.12)
The Good Samaritan (*Luke* 10)
The Workers in the Vineyard (*Matt.* 20)
The Quarrelling Quails (*Together Today* p. 220)
The Two Metre Chopsticks (*Together Today* p. 254)

Poem   The Mouse, the Frog and the Little Red Hen   Anon (CFM p. 19)

Songs   Kum ba yah (SSL no. 23)
I'd like to teach the world to sing (*Apusskidu* no. 2)
Cross over the road (CP no. 70)
The ink is black, the page is white (SSL no. 39)

Prayers 3, 34, 36, 48, 50, 63, 67, 69

Activities   Work together on some school, class or group project. Talk about ways in which your home, school or neighbourhood could be improved. Collect information e.g. press cuttings of any recent disaster and discuss how people working together have helped. Invite a speaker from a charity e.g. Oxfam, Christian Aid, Save the Children Fund to illustrate their world-wide work in helping others. Study animals working together e.g. ants and bees.

World Family

Theme   The people that we live with at home are called our family. Some members of our family may live far away, such as cousins, aunts or grandparents. All our families are just small parts of one big family, the world family, which is called the family of man. This family is so large we cannot possibly know everyone in it. It is made up of millions of people living in different countries all over the world. Sometimes people in families quarrel and get cross with each other. This happens in the world family too. We should try to make our world a happy family by showing that we love and care for others near at home and far away.

Stories   Folktales and legends from around the world

Poem   The World   W. B. Rands (*Book of a Thousand Poems* p. 421)

Songs   All the nations of the earth (CP no. 14)
The Building Song (CP no. 61)
In Christ there is no East or West (CP no. 66)
Black and White (CP no. 67)
The family of man (CP no. 69)

Prayers 17, 19, 26, 42, 44

Activities   Talk about, and show on a world map, the countries the children have visited. Show holiday pictures, postcards and souvenirs from different countries. Display dolls dressed in different costumes. Study different flag designs. Collect labels showing foods from different parts of the world. Look for coins and stamps from around the world.

Stories

Stories

The Ant and the Grasshopper 119
Baboushka 120
The Bundle of Sticks 121
The Cat who kept her Name 122
The Crow and the Jug 123
The Discontented Pig 124
The Fir Tree 125
The First Mirror 126
The First Silkworms 127
The First Snow 128
Five Little Fingers 129
Foolish Dan 130
The Four Fools 131
The Fox and the Crab 132
The Girl who liked watching Stars 133
Good King Wenceslas 134
The Goose that laid the Golden Eggs 135
The Happy Prince 136
How the Frog lost his Tail 137
How Jane found Friends 138
How the Tortoise got its Shell 139
How the Zebra got its Stripes 140
James and his Machines 141
The Jar of Ants 142
Jupiter and the Bee 143
Lazy Jack 144
The Lion and the Rabbit 145

The Lion who fell into a Hole 146
The Lost Sheep 147
The Magic Fish 148
The Man who said Thank You 149
The Man who sold his Shadow 150
Mary and her Bones 151
The Mean Beggar 152
The Milkmaid and her Pail 153
The Miller, the Son and the Donkey 154
The Monkey and her Baby 155
The Months of the Year 156
Not True! 157
The Parts of the Body 158
The Rich Man's Diamond 159
St Francis and the Wolf 160
St Jerome and the Lion 161
St Nicholas and the Gifts 162
St Valentine and the Blind Girl 163
The Shirt of Happiness 164
Solomon and the Baby 165
The Timid Hares 166
The Town Mouse and the Country Mouse 167
Why the Bat flies at Night 168
Why the Robin has a Red Breast 169
Why the Spider lives in a Web 170
The Young Man and the Swallow 171

The Ant and the Grasshopper

It was a fine summer day and the Grasshopper was chirping and singing as if he had not a care in the world. Just then an Ant passed by, struggling with a grain of corn which he was carrying to his nest.

The Grasshopper called out to the busy Ant, 'Come and play with me for a while. It is much too fine a day to be working.' The Ant looked at the Grasshopper. 'You do nothing but sing all day. I have not got time to sing and play. I must store up some food for the long winter days ahead. I suggest you do the same.' The Grasshopper laughed and said, 'Why worry about the winter? I have enough food to eat now.' And he went on singing.

The months passed. The snows of winter lay on the fields. One cold, frosty day the Ant came out of his nest to dry some grains of corn which had grown damp during the wet autumn weather. Along came the Grasshopper, half dead with cold and hunger. 'Please give me some corn from your store, for I have no food to eat,' said the Grasshopper.

'You should have gathered it last summer,' said the Ant. 'We worked day and night to get this corn in. We have enough to last all winter. Why should we give it to you?'

Without another word the Ant went back to his work, and the Grasshopper went away a sadder but wiser insect.

Baboushka

It was Christmas Eve, many years ago. The night was cold and dark, with one bright star shining in the East. An old woman named Baboushka sat in her snug little house by a warm fire. She was just dropping off to sleep in her rocking chair when she heard a knock on the door. Slowly she went to open it, and there stood three men dressed in fine clothes. In their hands they were holding precious gifts.

'I am Melchior,' said the first man. 'We have travelled far, Baboushka, following a great star in the East. We have stopped to tell you of the Baby Prince born in Bethlehem. Will you come with us to see him?' Baboushka shook her head. Then the second man stepped forward. 'I am Gaspar,' he said. 'We are taking gifts to the Baby Jesus. Will you come with us?' Baboushka thought for a while, but again shook her head. The third stranger then spoke. 'I am Balthasar,' he said. 'We go to worship the baby born this night who is to be king and lord of all. Come with us, Baboushka.'

Baboushka thought once more, and said, 'Yes, I would like to see the Baby Jesus and bring him a gift. You go on, good sirs, and I will catch you up.' So the three Wise Men went on their way following the star to Bethlehem. Baboushka put on her hat and coat, and then thought of all the things she should do to the house. She liked everything to be neat and tidy. So she began to clean and dust, and put things away. By the time she had finished it was very late. 'I will go and visit him tomorrow,' she said. 'When it is light I shall take him a gift of some toys.'

But in the morning when she looked for the star it was gone. There was no trace of the Wise Men, and she did not know which way to go. So Baboushka with her basket full of toys set off to try to find the Baby Jesus. They say that old Baboushka is still looking, and every Christmas Eve when children are fast asleep she leaves a toy from her basket for every child—in the hope that one day she will find the Baby Jesus.

The Bundle of Sticks

There was once a father who had a family four sons. He loved his four sons, and they loved him. The only trouble was that the four sons were always quarrelling and squabbling among themselves. He was always telling them how much happier life would be if they worked together but they took no notice of him. He tried in every way to teach them to get along but they still quarrelled. So one day father decided to show the boys what he meant.

He called his sons together and said, 'I have got something special to show you.' Then he put a bundle of sticks on the floor in front of them. The bundle had been tied tightly together with string.

'Can you break that?' he asked the youngest son. The boy pressed and pulled with all his strength but he could not even bend it. The father asked each son in turn to try to break the bundle, but none of them could do it.

Then he untied the string and separated the sticks. He gave a stick to each son. 'Now try,' he said. And each son broke his stick easily. 'Do you see what I mean?' said the father. 'If only you stay together like this bundle of sticks, then you will be strong and no one can hurt you. But if you disagree and quarrel all the time, and go your separate ways, our family will be broken just like we have broken these sticks.'

So the four boys learned their lesson. In future they tried to work and play together, as a family. It did not always work, but when it did they were all much happier. And so was their father.

The Cat who kept her Name

'Oh, I wish I were someone else,' said the cat. So the first thing she decided to do was to go off and find herself a new name. As she was walking through a wood she met a tiger.

'Excuse me,' said the cat. 'You are strong and brave. May I call myself "Tiger"?'

'Of course,' said the tiger. 'It is the best name there is.'

'It is not as good as my name,' said a fiery voice. The cat looked round and saw a large, ugly dragon. The tiger ran off as fast as he could. The cat looked at the dragon.

'Yes, I think yours is a better name. May I call myself "Dragon"?' said the cat.

'Of course,' said the dragon. 'It is the best name there is.'

Then a large cloud appeared and it began to rain. The fine dragon soon looked wet and bedraggled, and hid under a tree.

'Oh cloud, you are stronger than the dragon. May I take your name?' aked the cat.

'Good idea,' said the cloud. 'But I must go now before the wind blows me away.'

'Perhaps "Wind" is a better name,' said the cat.

'I can stop any wind,' said the wall. 'Mine is the strongest name of all.'

'In that case I shall call myself "Wall",' said the cat.

'No wall can stop me,' said a squeaky voice, from a hole in the wall. A small nose and whiskers peeped out. 'A rat is better than any wall,' said the voice. 'Call yourself "Rat", it is the best name of all.'

Slowly the cat crept closer to the hole in the wall. The rat looked to see who was there and the cat pounced. 'Got you!' said the cat.

'Let me go! Let me go!' squeaked the rat, but it was too late. 'Now I know the best name of all,' said the cat. 'The dragon was stronger than the tiger, but his name was not best. Nor was the cloud's, nor the wind's, nor the wall's, nor the rat's. Now I have you under my paw. The best name for me is just—Cat.'

The cat was so pleased to have found the best name that he let the rat go. And ever since cats have been very pleased to be just cats.

The Crow and the Jug

One hot summer day a crow was looking for some water to drink. There had been no rain for several weeks and he was almost dying of thirst. All the puddles and ponds he usually drank from had dried up. The poor crow did not know what to do.

At last he saw a tall jug standing outside the back door of a house. He stretched up and looked inside. In the bottom of the jug he saw what he was looking for—water! But try as he might he could not reach the water with his beak. How could he get at it?

'Perhaps if I knock it over I could break the top off,' he thought. He tried to push the jug, but it was too heavy. He tried pecking it with his beak, but nothing happened. Then he saw some small stones lying nearby, and had an idea.

The crow picked up a pebble in his beak and dropped it into the jug. The water rose a tiny bit. Then he took another pebble and dropped that in. The water rose a little bit more. One by one he dropped in all the pebbles. Gradually the pebbles filled the bottom of the jug, pushing the water higher and higher. When he had dropped in a hundred pebbles the water at last rose near to the top. The crow was now able to dip his tired beak into the cool water and drink his fill.

The Discontented Pig

There was once a pig who lived on his own in a small cottage near a village. He was a keen gardener. He planted seeds and grew juicy vegetables and the most beautiful flowers. People came from miles around to buy his produce. At the local show his plants and vegetables won nearly all the prizes. Every day the pig could be seen digging or weeding or hoeing or planting. He was a very good gardener.

After a few years the pig grew tired of all the hard work involved in growing vegetables. 'There must be an easier way of earning a living,' he said. 'I think I'll go and find a better job.' So off he went.

Soon he came to a cottage where he heard the sound of sweet music. It was Tinkerbell, a cat who made a good living by playing the violin. 'If a cat can play a fiddle then I can,' thought the pig. 'Being a musician must be easier than my job.'

'Will you teach me to play?' asked the pig.

'Of course,' said the cat. 'All you need is to practise five hours a day for the next few years and you'll become a good musician.'

'Five hours a day!' said the pig. 'I don't think I'll bother, thank you. Goodbye.'

Next he came to the house of a dog who made cheese. There was the dog stirring a large bucket of milk. 'Will you show me how to make cheese?' said the pig. 'I am sure it is easier than my job.'

'Certainly,' said the dog. 'Take this spoon and stir as fast as you can until the cheese is formed.'

The pig took the spoon and began to stir. After a while his arms were aching and he stopped for a rest. 'You mustn't stop,' said the dog, 'or you will spoil the cheese.'

'My arms are dropping off!' said the pig. 'Goodbye.'

Next he saw a bee-keeper taking honey out of his beehives. 'I'm sure being a bee-keeper is easier than my job,' said the pig. 'Will you teach me to be a bee-keeper?'

'Of course,' said the bee-keeper. 'Just take out that honeycomb from the beehive.' The pig bent down and carefully picked up the honeycomb. At once several bees flew out and stung him on the face. The pig screamed with pain and ran away. 'Come back,' shouted the man. 'If you want to be a bee-keeper you must put up with a few stings.'

'No thanks,' said the pig, who ran right back to his own little cottage. Soon he was busy again working on the vegetables in his own garden. And for the first time in a long while he felt really happy—just growing things in his own garden.

The Fir Tree

Once in the woods there grew a little fir tree. Its leaves were long, slender green needles. But the little fir tree did not like its long sharp leaves. 'I wish I had different leaves,' it said. 'I would like leaves that were better than any other tree—leaves of shining gold.'

It so happened that an angel overheard what the fir tree said, and when the fir tree woke the next morning its leaves had turned to shining gold. 'How beautiful I am,' said the fir tree. 'Look how my leaves shine in the sun. All the other trees look so dull beside me.'

Foolish little fir tree! That night a man crept into the woods with a bag. He went straight to the fir tree, picked off all his gold leaves and took them home in his bag.

Next morning the fir tree felt very sad. 'I won't wish for gold leaves again,' he said. 'But if I had glass leaves, they too would sparkle in the sun. I wish I could have leaves of glass.' Again the angel heard the fir tree's words, and in the morning the fir tree sparkled with shiny glass leaves. However, that afternoon dark clouds hid the sun, the thunder rolled and rain came pouring down. A strong wind blew and soon the fir tree's glass leaves came crashing down. When the storm had passed all that was left was broken glass at the foot of the fir tree.

'Oh, I wish I could have nice green leaves like the other trees,' said the fir tree. 'I would be happy then.' The angel heard him, and when morning came the fir tree was covered in large green leaves. But soon a hungry goat came walking by, saw the big juicy leaves and ate every one up for his dinner. Poor little fir tree! A man had taken his leaves of gold, the wind had broken his leaves of glass and now a goat had eaten all his green leaves. What could he wish for now?

'If only I had my long green needles back again!' sighed the little fir tree. Once again the angel heard his words, and the next morning the fir tree was covered again in long green needles. The birds soon flew to him to build their nests in his arms. When winter came and the leaves fell from other trees, they stayed safe and warm in the little fir tree.

'There is nothing better than my own green needles,' said the fir tree. And the angel of the forest smiled.

The First Mirror

A story about how the first mirror came to Japan.

One day a young farmer was on his way home after a hard day's work in the fields when out of the corner of his eye he saw something glinting by the roadside. It was a piece of shining glass. He picked it up and looked at it carefully. To his surprise he saw the face of a handsome young man staring at him. 'What a wonderful picture,' he thought. 'I will take it back home with me.' So he put it into his bag and continued on his way.

When he got home his wife was cooking the evening meal so he left his bag in the corner and sat down at the table. While the young man was eating his wife decided to put his bag away. Inside the bag she noticed the mirror. So she took it out and looked at it. To her surprise she saw a picture of a beautiful young woman. 'Husband,' she said, 'why are you keeping a picture of a woman in your bag?'

'Don't be silly, wife,' said the husband. 'It is a picture of a man. I found it by the roadside.'

'That is no man,' said the wife looking into the mirror again. 'It is a woman. Tell me, who is she?' The husband was sure that the mirror was a picture of a man, and his wife was sure that it was a woman, so they fell to arguing. They were arguing so loudly that an old priest heard them as he was walking by. The woman was shouting at the man, and the man in an even louder voice was shouting at the woman. So the old man knocked on their door to see if he could help.

'Come in,' said the wife. 'You can settle this argument for us. My husband says this is a picture of a man, and I say it is a picture of a woman. Look, and say which one of us is right.' She handed the old man the mirror and he looked closely at it. 'You are both wrong,' he said. 'This is a picture of a wise old man.' The husband and wife stopped in amazement. 'Let me take it,' said the old priest. 'It is the picture of a very holy man, probably a saint. I will hang it up in the temple where it belongs.' So the priest carried the mirror to the temple. It was the first time the people had seen a mirror and they were fascinated by it. When the sun shone on it the mirror shone like the sun. And each person who looked into the mirror saw something different, but none of them argued quite so much as the husband and wife who had found the first mirror.

The First Silkworms

Many years ago in China there lived a beautiful princess. No one knows her name, but we do know that she loved playing in the palace garden. It was a beautiful garden with flowers, trees and birds of every kind. There were ponds full of goldfish with little red bridges arching over them. No wonder it was her favourite place.

One day in the garden the princess saw some strange worms feeding on the leaves of a mulberry tree. Each day the worms grew bigger, and she showed them to her friends. Then the weather grew wet and cold, and the princess had to stay inside the palace. But on the next sunny day she went out again to look at the strange worms.

To her surprise the princess saw that the worms had stopped eating, and were covering themselves in white oval-shaped cases. 'Oh dear,' thought the princess. 'The poor worms have eaten too much. They are dying and making their own little coffins to be buried in.' The princess gathered the cocoons and dug a little grave for them under the mulberry tree. 'We must give them a proper funeral,' she said. So she ordered her servant to fetch tea and rice cakes, like they did at proper Chinese funerals. Then she dropped the cocoons, one by one, into the grave.

The last cocoon, however, slipped out of her fingers, and dropped into the princess's cup of tea. When she picked it out she found it had become soft, and a thread as fine as a cobweb had come loose. 'Oh dear,' she said, 'this little worm's coffin is coming to pieces.' The princess was so upset she ran in and told her mother what had happened. Her mother, the Empress, looked carefully at the cocoon, and then slowly began to unwind one long glistening thread. This gave the Empress an idea.

'Show me where you found those worms,' said the Empress. So the princess led her to the mulberry tree where she saw some more worms spinning their cocoons. 'Daughter, you have found something truly wonderful. From this thread we shall weave the most beautiful cloth in the world.' And that is how the first silk cloth came to be woven. All because of a little girl who found some strange worms in her garden.

(Chinese legend)

The First Snow

The New Year falls in the middle of winter when the earth is bleak and bare. The cold winds blew. No vegetables grew in the frosty ground, and there was no fruit on the trees. There was little food to eat, and the people were hungry and miserable. As the gods looked down they were sad to see how the people suffered. So they threw great handfuls of flour from the heavens which the poor people could collect and make into cakes.

Each New Year clouds of flour came floating down. The people gathered up the flour and soon there was the smell of baking everywhere. Even in the harshest weather the people had enough to eat and the gods were pleased.

For several winters the plan worked well. But soon the people began to take the flour for granted. They grew lazy. All work stopped when the flour came drifting down. They even began to call for more flour, so that they could work even less. Finally they began to quarrel over it, and steal it from each other. Poor people became mean and selfish, and began many fights. The rich were even worse. They paid men to gather as much flour as they could for themselves, then sold it to the poor for high prices.

The gods were angry at the evil they saw, and tried to think of a way to punish mankind. So when next it was time for the flour to fall, they turned it into ice, and sent down freezing white flakes of snow to cleanse the hearts of ungrateful men.

And so at the time when families are baking their New Year cakes there is often a fall of snow, and this reminds them of the first snow that fell many years ago.

(Chinese legend)

Five Little Fingers

Hold out your right hand. What do you see? A round bit called the palm of your hand, and five little fingers. On the left is the Little Finger. He's the smallest of the five. In America they call him the Pinkie. He is not a very strong finger. In fact there is very little that he can do on his own. Some people used to stretch out the little finger when holding a teacup. They thought it was the polite thing to do.

Next to him is the Feeble Finger. He is called this because he is so weak. He finds it very difficult to move without some of the other fingers helping him. If you try waggling him backwards and forwards you will see what I mean.

The next finger along is Middle Finger. He is the tallest of them all, but he too cannot do much by himself.

Then comes Index Finger. He is the busiest of all the fingers. He is good at pointing and pressing and pulling and picking things up. He's the one people often use when they say, 'Come here,' or, 'Go over there.' The Index Finger is sometimes wagged at you when you get told off. He is sometimes called the forefinger—perhaps this is because he is the fourth finger along.

Last of all comes old Thumb. Though he is short he is a tough little fellow. He's the strongest finger of all, good for pushing things in like drawing pins. People sometimes stick him in the air to say that everything is all right.

None of these five little fingers can do much by himself. But when they work together, and help each other, they can do wonderful things. They can paint pictures, play music, throw and catch, and make many interesting models. They can do important jobs for us like tying laces, doing up buttons, and using a knife and fork. They can do nice things like stroking, tickling and holding hands. Fingers are rather like people; they cannot do much on their own but when they work together there are so many good things that they can do.

Foolish Dan

There was once a boy named Dan who lived with his mother in a hut in the woods. They were a poor family and one day there was no more food left in the house. Dan's mother said, 'All we have left is this bag of seeds. Take them to market and sell them. Then with the money you can buy some food.'

So Dan took the bag of seeds and set off for market, but soon Dan forgot all about what his mother said. It was a hot day. 'I wish I had a hat,' said Dan, 'to shade my head.' Just then a man came along the road. He had a big hat on his head. 'Good day,' said Dan. 'I wonder if you would let me have your hat for these seeds.' The man agreed, for the seeds were worth much more than his old hat.

Off went Dan towards the woods, and forgot all about going to market and buying food for his mother. After a while he began to feel thirsty, so he sat under a tree and fanned himself with his hat. Soon an old woman came by with a jug of water. 'Good day,' said Dan. 'Would you give me your jug of water in exchange for this hat?' The old woman liked the look of the hat so she gave Dan the jug of water, and went on her way with his hat.

Dan drank all the water and walked on through the wood singing to himself and swinging the empty jug in his hand. He had forgotten all about the market and what he had been sent to do. Soon he began to feel hungry. How could he find something to eat? Just then he saw a boy coming towards him eating an apple. 'Good day,' said Dan. 'May I have the rest of your apple in exchange for this jug? I am very hungry.' The boy saw the jug had some value, and gave Dan his apple.

Dan soon ate the apple, and still felt hungry. 'I think I'll go home now,' he thought. 'Mother is sure to find me something to eat.' When he got home his mother said, 'Have you sold the seeds? What food have brought home from market?'

'Oh dear,' said Dan. 'I forgot!'

'You forgot? You forgot? I'll teach you not to forget,' said his mother. Foolish Dan's mother picked up the rolling pin and chased him from the house. Dan went to bed a very hungry boy that night.

(Old English folktale)

The Four Fools

One day four men went out in a boat. Each man was a fool. They were going fishing. After a while one of them stood up, and the boat began to rock. 'What are you standing up for?' asked one of the other men.

'I am looking for fish,' said the man. A second man stood up and the boat began to rock more. It is strange how if one person is looking at something everyone wants to have a look. Soon the third man stood up. The boat rocked wildly to and fro. Then the fourth man stood up. Over went the boat, and the four fools fell into the water.

Luckily each man could swim, so they swam to the shore. 'Are we all safe?' asked one of the men. 'I don't know. You had better count us,' said another. 'One, two, three,' counted the first fool. But he had forgotten to count himself. 'Oh dear!' he said. 'One of us has drowned.'

'Let me count,' said another fool. 'One, two, three.' He also forgot to count himself. 'You are right. One of us has drowned. How sad!' And the four fools began to cry for their lost friend.

Just then a young man came by. 'What is the matter?' he asked. 'Our friend has drowned in the river,' said one of the fools. 'There were four of us in the boat, and now there are only three. One, two, three!'

'I see,' said the young man. 'Perhaps I can help you. If I can find your friend, would you give me some gold as a reward?'

'Oh yes,' said the four fools. 'We will give you our gold, if only you can find our friend.'

'Well, here he is,' said the young man. He hit the first fool on the head. 'One,' he said. Then he hit the second fool. 'Two.' He hit the third. 'Three.' And he hit the fourth. 'Four. There is your friend!'

The fools were happy because their friend had been found. The young man was happy because he had his gold. So they were all happy—all five of them.

The Fox and the Crab

One day a fox said to a crab, 'Tell me, litle crawling thing, do you know how to run?'

'Oh yes,' said the crab. 'I often run from the mud to the grass, and back to the river.'

'That is not very far,' said the fox. 'How many feet and legs have you?'

'Eight, I think,' said the crab. 'Just let me count.'

'I have only four,' said the fox. 'Why, if I had as many as you have I would run at least six times as fast as you. You really are a very slow and stupid creature. I never heard of anyone with so many feet running so slowly.'

The crab said, 'Would you like to have a race with me? As you are ten times larger than I am you will have to run ten times faster. Besides, you have a large tail and you hold it so high that it makes you run faster. If you would allow me to put it down I don't think you could run any faster than I.'

'Oh, very well,' said the proud fox, 'do as you like. I shall win without even trying. No creature in the forest is as fast as I am, and none is as clever. So do as you like, silly crab.'

'I will hang something on to your tail to hold it down,' said the crab. 'When I say "Go", the race will start.'

So the crab caught the fox's tail in his pincers and said, 'Ready ... Go!' The fox ran and ran until he was tired out, with the crab still holding on to his tail. When he stopped, there was the crab beside him.

'I thought you said you were faster than I?' said the crab. 'But you are not one step ahead with all your boasting.' The fox, panting for breath, hung his head in shame. Never again would he boast that he was faster or cleverer than any other animal—just in case they asked him for a race. And he went where he might never see the crab again.

(Indian folktale)

The Girl who liked watching Stars

Maria Mitchell was an ordinary little girl except for one thing—she loved looking at the stars. At night when the sky was clear she would climb up to the attic and gaze through the attic window at the stars. They were like jewels that flashed and twinkled and made bright patterns. But Maria's mother did not like it. 'Maria, come down from the attic at once,' she called. 'A little girl shouldn't spend so much time looking at the stars.'

Maria's father didn't mind. In fact her interest pleased him. One day he gave Maria a telescope so that she could see the stars better. She took it up to the attic and looked through it—the stars shone bigger and brighter than ever.

Now she had a telescope, Maria grew more and more interested in watching the stars. One night her father told her to look out for a comet, which is a kind of shooting star. 'A comet!' said Maria. 'How wonderful!' 'If you look carefully,' said her father, 'you will see a bright light moving across the sky. It will have a long tail. There are not many comets in the sky. If you see a new one you might become famous.'

So night after night Maria searched the skies. But it was a long time before she saw what she was looking for. Then one night Maria saw something marvellous through the telescope. It was very late, when she should have been fast asleep—half past ten on October 1st in 1847, Maria saw a flash of light. It looked like a star, except it was moving through space. It had a long tail. It was a new comet and Maria was the first person to see it.

For her find the King of Denmark gave her a gold medal, and a gift of money. Soon the whole world had heard of Maria's discovery. She became famous. When she grew up she learned a lot more science. She became a teacher, and even wrote books about the stars. And it all started when she was a little girl who loved watching stars.

Good King Wenceslas

There was a once a page boy who sat warming himself by the fire in the kitchen of a great castle. His job was to run errands for his master, the king. But now he was feeling warm and rather sleepy. 'Wake up! Wake up!' said the cook. 'King Wenceslas wants you—so you had better hurry!'

Quickly the boy ran to the king's chamber, and found the king sitting by a window. 'Come here, page, and stand by me,' he said. The page boy went to the king's side and looked out into the night. There was deep snow everywhere, sparkling in the moonlight. The king pointed to a man walking across the snow. 'That poor old man. Who is he? And where does he live?' asked the king.

'Sir, he lives in a hut at the foot of the mountain. It's against the forest fence, by St Agnes' fountain.'

'That poor man looks cold and hungry,' said the king. 'We must go and help him. Bring me meat and wine and fetch me some pine logs. You and I will take a dinner to that old man tonight.'

Soon everything was ready. The king carried a bag of food under his cloak, and a lantern in his hand. The page boy picked up a bundle of pine logs, and out they walked into the night. A bitter wind blew, and snowflakes whirled around them. 'We'll soon be there,' said the king. What a long way it seemed. The page boy's hands and feet were freezing cold as he struggled on through the deep snow. 'Sir, the night is getting dark, and the wind grows stronger. I don't think I can go on any longer.'

King Wenceslas turned round. 'Walk behind me,' he said, 'and I will protect you from the wind. Put your feet in my footprints and perhaps you will not feel so cold.' So the page boy walked behind the king and stepped in his footprints. As he did so his feet began to feel warmer. It was like a game, the king leading and the page boy following in his footsteps.

They soon reached the old man's hut. And you can imagine how surprised the old man was when he opened his door, to find a king and his page boy bringing him their gifts on that cold St Stephen's night.

The Goose that laid the Golden Eggs

One morning a farmer was amazed to find that his goose had laid a golden egg. He picked up the precious egg and ran into the house to tell his wife. 'Look, wife,' he said, 'We are rich! We are rich!' The farmer then took the golden egg and sold it for a good price.

The next morning the goose laid another golden egg. The farmer sold that, too, for much money. Every day the goose laid an egg of purest gold. One by one the farmer sold the eggs. But the richer the farmer and his wife became, the more money they wanted.

One day the farmer's wife said to her husband, 'These eggs are all very well, my dear, but it is a slow way of becoming rich. Why should we be content with only one egg a day? I have an idea. There must be a great many golden eggs inside our goose. Why not kill the goose and cut her open, then we can have all the golden eggs at once?'

The farmer agreed. Without another word he killed the goose and cut her open—but alas, there was no gold at all inside. So because they had been greedy, the farmer and his wife had no more golden eggs—and no goose, either.

(Aesop)

The Happy Prince

In the autumn, when the days turn colder, most of our birds fly off to spend winter in warmer lands. One autumn a swallow set out later than his friends and as he flew south he came to a big city. In the centre of this city was a golden statue. The swallow flew up and had a close look at it. It was the statue of a splendid person holding a sword. The figure was covered in gold, with a jewel on its sword and sparkling jewels for eyes. To his surprise, the swallow saw that the statue had tears in its eyes.

'Who are you?' asked the swallow.

'I am the Happy Prince,' answered the statue. 'At least, that is what people called me when I was alive. I was the prince of this city and lived in a fine palace. I never knew how the poor people of my city lived. When I died they made this magnificent statue you see before you. But now I see how poor and miserable many of my people are and I can do nothing to help them. That is why I am crying.'

'How sad!' said the swallow. 'Perhaps I can help you.'

'I can see an old woman with a sick child in a room across the city. She needs money to buy food to make her child well. Will you pluck the jewel from my sword and take it to her?'

The days were getting cold and the swallow knew that he was late, but he said he would help. He took the jewel from the sword and flew to the old woman's room and left it on her table. The next morning as he was about to fly away, the Happy Prince asked the swallow to do one more thing for him. It was to take a jewel from the Happy Prince's eye and give it to a poor writer who had no money for food or a fire.

The next day the Happy Prince begged the swallow to stay one day longer. 'There is a poor girl,' he said, 'who sells matches for a living. She has dropped them all in the gutter. When she gets home her father will beat her. Please take her my other eye-jewel.' 'But you will be blind,' said the swallow. 'Never mind that,' said the statue. 'Will you do it?'

'Yes, but this must be my last trip,' said the swallow. 'The frosts are coming and I am very late.' So he took the last jewel to the little matchgirl, and changed her tears into smiles.

The next day the Happy Prince asked the swallow to take off the gold from his statue to give to the poor people of the city. Day after day the swallow took bits of the statue and gave them to all those who were poor or hungry.

By now it was too late for the swallow to go. He was too cold and weak to fly. He said a final goodbye to the Happy Prince. The statue now looked old and shabby without its gold covering, and so it was pulled down. The heart of the Happy Prince was thrown on a dustheap where it lay next to the body of the swallow.

(Adapted from Oscar Wilde)

How the Frog lost his Tail

Frog sat in his muddy home at the edge of the pond and felt miserable. He knew he was ugly, with a mouth like a black cave, eyes which stuck out like doorknobs and a green shiny body. But what made the Frog saddest of all was that he had no tail.

Each evening Frog watched the forest animals come down to the pond to drink. They all had long swishy tails, except for Frog. So Frog went to the Sky God and said, 'I am so ugly. Please give me a tail.'

'Very well,' boomed the Sky God in a voice like thunder. 'I will give you a tail if you will be a watchman at my special well and see that it never dries up.' Frog agreed to watch over the well, and the Sky God gave him a tail.

Frog made himself a new home beside the special well and spent the time hopping to and fro, showing off his fine long tail. Frog now thought himself the handsomest creature in the whole world. Having such a magnificent tail made him very proud and bossy. The animals kept well away from the unfriendly frog.

Unfortunately all the other ponds and wells dried up except for the special well which was guarded by Frog. When the animals crawled weakly towards him in search of water, Frog would say, 'Who is coming to the special well?' The animals would say their names and ask him for water. Then frog would shout: 'Go away! Go away! There is no water here. The well is dry.'

At last the animals told the Sky God of Frog's behaviour. So he thought he would go himself to see what was happening. As he came close to the well Frog shouted, 'Go away! Go away! There's no water here. The well is dry.' The Sky God shook with anger, and decided to punish the unkind frog. So he took away his tail and sent him back to his pond.

Each year the Sky God reminds Frog of the misery he caused. In spring when the Frog is born as a tadpole he has a long, beautiful tail. But as he grows, his tail shrinks and shrinks until it finally disappears.

The Sky God takes the tail away because Frog was once so selfish and spiteful.

(African legend)

How Jane found Friends

The children at school did not like Jane. She was always fighting and she never shared her toys. Poor Jane had no mother or father. She lived with her aunt, but her aunt did not bother much about her. Jane often went home from school to an empty house and a cold tea.

The real trouble with Jane was that she was always boasting about the fine things she had. She did not really have them. She just wished she had them—and told others that she had. But the children at school got tired of hearing her boasting. So they began to argue and to fight with her. And no one wanted to be friends with Jane.

One day as she was walking home her school bag came open, and out fell all her books. It was a rainy day and the ground was wet. Poor Jane started to cry. The twins in her class, Peter and Anne, were behind her, and they stopped to help. Carefully they picked Jane's books up from the ground. Oh dear, they were wet! 'Don't cry,' said Anne. 'We will carry them to your house. It is not far from where we live.'

For once Jane did not argue or fight. All three children went to Jane's house. Of course there was no one at home. The twins felt sorry for Jane. 'Why don't you come home with us?' said Peter. 'We can all have tea together.' So that is what Jane did.

From that day on Jane felt much happier. Each afternoon when school had finished she went home with the twins. They read stories together or played games. Then they had their tea. Jane no longer had to pretend about the good things she had, for she now had two wonderful friends. And that was the truth.

How the Tortoise got its Shell

Once the tortoise was like other animals. He did not have a shell as he does now. But that was long ago. It happened like this ...

The lion was going to have a party. He was the king of the jungle and it was his birthday. So he invited all the animals to come to a feast. There were elephants and rhinoceroses, kangaroos and koala bears, monkeys and mice, ostriches and eagles, crocodiles and cobra snakes—in fact, every kind of animal you can think of. All, that is, except the tortoise. He was the only one who did not go to the party.

The lion was angry. The next time he saw the tortoise he said, 'Hello friend tortoise. Why did you not come to my party?'

'Because I stayed at home,' said the tortoise. 'I have such a nice home, I don't like going out.'

'If you like your home so much,' said the lion, 'you had better go there and stay there. If I see you out again, I shall eat you for my dinner!'

The tortoise was scared by the lion's words. And from that day on he never left his home. The tortoise carries a hard shell on his back wherever he goes. Wherever he is, he is always at home.

How the Zebra got its Stripes

When God had made all the animals, in the morning of time, he told them all to go and work. 'You must help each other,' said God. 'If you work together you will be happy.'

One of the animals that God made was the zebra. At that time the zebra had a coat which was shining white all over. And God said to the zebra, 'Go and work for man, like your brother the horse.' But the zebra was lazy; he did not want to pull a plough or to carry man from place to place on his back. So he pretended to go and work, but went off and hid instead in a forest of tall bamboo trees.

But the eyes of God see all, and he could see the Zebra hiding among the bamboo trees. And God was angry. 'Oh Zebra,' he said, 'you have not done what I asked. You have not helped man, but have hidden yourself away. Lazy creature, as a punishment your coat shall no longer be white. From now on it shall be marked with the shadows of the bamboo trees.' And so it was. From that day on the zebra's coat was covered in stripes.

When night falls in the forest no one can see the zebra because his stripes make him invisible. But when daylight comes the lion can see him easily from far off, and can hunt and catch him. That is the price the zebra pays for being so lazy, and not working with man.

(African legend)

James and his Machines

James was a little boy who always liked making things. Most of all he liked to make models that worked. Luckily James's father, Mr Watt, was a carpenter and he let James come into his workshop. There James made his models, out of wood and string and bits of metal.

One day two men came over to see what James was making. 'Look!' said one of the men. 'Look at what the little boy has made!' James had made a toy crane. It was only a model, but it looked like a big crane. And it worked like a big crane. He had made a machine that worked and he was still only five years old.

Later when James was grown up he saw another model. This one had been made by someone else. It was a model of a steam engine. James had been fascinated as a boy to see how hard the steam blew from the spout of a boiling kettle—and how hot it was. Now on this model the steam was being used to push a wheel round. It was not a very good machine for the wheel kept stopping. So James tried to repair it, but even he could not make it work for long.

But James did not give up. He made up his mind that he would build a steam machine that worked properly. He did not have much money and life was a struggle for him. Time and again he built a model of a machine, only to find that it broke down. At last he built a good machine. First of all he made a small model which worked and then he built a big version of it. People saw how well it worked, and they bought James Watt's steam engines for their mines and factories. The boy who made models was now famous.

Soon there were steam engines all over Britain. New factories were built and Britain became one of the richest countries in the world. Looking at James Watt's steam engine gave people other ideas, too. What would happen, they said, if you put a steam engine on wheels? They tried it, but that's another story.

The Jar of Ants

One evening a man hurried home to his wife and said, 'I have just heard that on that nearby mountain there is a large tree, and under that tree a jar of gold is buried. I thought of digging it up this evening, but I'm rather tired. I think I'll go to bed early tonight and dig it up first thing tomorrow morning.'

Next door there lived a nosy neighbour. He loved to know everybody's business. With his ear to the wall he could hear every word that the man said. He rubbed his hands with glee at the thought of the gold. And at once he rushed off to dig up the jar.

He soon found the one large tree on the mountainside, and began digging. Clink! His spade hit a heavy jar. Carefully he lifted it out of the earth and reached inside for the gold. But to his horror he found something very different—ants!

The man was hopping mad. He covered up the jar and ran back to the house of the husband and wife. Once there he climbed up on to their roof, and loosened several tiles. Through the gap he could see the bed where they were sleeping. Over the bed they had hung a net to protect them from mosquitoes. Fortunately there was a hole in the net. This suited the man's plan perfectly. He shouted, 'You lied to me, so here are the ants for you to eat.' Then he emptied the jar though the hole—but all he could hear was the sound of falling money.

This woke the husband. 'Amazing!' he said. 'Gold is raining down from heaven.' Their bed was covered in gold coins.

Up on the roof the neighbour stared into the jar—it was empty.

(Chinese folktale)

Jupiter and the Bee

Jupiter was the king of the gods and he lived high on Mount Olympus. Each year Jupiter was given presents by his animal friends, and in return Jupiter helped the animals whenever he could.

The Queen Bee wondered what gift she should give to Jupiter. Of course—honey! She collected the freshest honey from her honeycombs and flew with it up to Jupiter's home on Mount Olympus. When Jupiter had opened his present and tasted the sweet honey he was so pleased that he said, 'Queen Bee, tell me what you would like. Whatever you wish shall be yours.'

'Oh, Jupiter,' said the Queen Bee, 'there is one thing that I would like. Give me a sting so that I may kill whoever comes near my hive to steal my honey.'

Jupiter was shocked that the Queen Bee would want such a spiteful wish. But he could not take back his promise. So he said, 'You shall have your sting. And when you attack anyone who takes your honey you may give them a nasty sting.'

The Queen Bee was about to thank Jupiter. But he held up his hand and said, 'The sting that you have will kill—but it will only kill you. Once you use your sting, it shall be torn from you, and you will die from the loss of it.'

And so the Queen Bee learnt that if you wish to hurt others you will end up by hurting yourself.

(Aesop)

Lazy Jack

Jack was a lazy boy. He lived with his mother in a little tumbledown cottage. They were very poor. Jack had no father, and his mother worked hard every day, spinning wool. But Jack never lifted a finger to help her. He just sat around all day in a rocking chair, if he wasn't still snoozing in his bed. No wonder they called him Lazy Jack.

One day his mother said to him, 'If you don't find a job by tomorrow I'll throw you out of the house. So off you go, and don't come back till you find one.' Lazy Jack went to a neighbouring farmer who gave him a job for a day. That evening the farmer gave Jack a £1 note for his work. On the way home Jack took the note out to look at it. Just then a gust of wind blew the note out of his hand and he lost it.

His mother was very angry. 'You should have put it into your pocket,' she said.

'I'll do it next time,' said Lazy Jack.

The next day Jack helped in a dairy, and he was given a jug of milk to take home with him. Remembering what his mother said he poured the milk into his pocket. When he got home his mother was even more angry. 'You should have carried it on your head!' she shouted.

'I'll do that next time,' said Lazy Jack.

Next day Jack got a job with another farmer, and was given a large packet of butter for helping him. Jack set off home with the butter carefully balanced on his head. It was very sunny that day and the butter began to melt. Gradually it ran down his hair and neck until he was covered in it. 'You silly boy,' screamed his mother. 'You should have carried it under your coat!'

'I'll do it next time,' said Lazy Jack.

Next day Jack worked for a farmer who gave him a donkey for helping. Jack picked the animal up and tried to put it under his coat. Holding on to the struggling donkey Jack headed for home. On his way home Jack passed the house of an unhappy girl who had never laughed in her life. No one could even make her smile. But when she saw Jack trying to hold a donkey under his jacket she rubbed her eyes in amazement. First she smiled, then she began to laugh.

Lazy Jack fell in love with the laughing girl and they soon got married. Jack promised her from that day he would work hard and stop his lazy ways. And they never called him Lazy Jack again.

The Lion and the Rabbit

There was once a cruel lion who enjoyed killing all the animals that came his way, whether he was hungry or not. So the animals met to discuss the matter. If the lion carried on like this there would soon be no animals left in the forest. What could they do? The mongoose had an idea. 'Let us offer the lion one animal, a different kind each day, otherwise he will kill us all.'

The animals agreed, and each day a different animal was chosen to feed the lion. At last came the turn of the rabbits, and they chose the oldest of their kind—old Greybeard. Greybeard was a wise old rabbit. He took his time, nibbling here and there in the bushes. As the lion waited he grew more and more angry.

'Where is that rabbit who is supposed to be coming?' he roared. 'If he is not here soon I shall kill all the animals of the forest. How dare they disobey me, the King of the Beasts!'

Just then the rabbit appeared. The lion pounced. 'Got you!' he growled. 'Take pity on me, great king,' whimpered Greybeard. 'I would have been here before, but on the way I met another lion who told me he was the King of the Beasts. I only just managed to escape.'

'What?' he roared. 'Is there another lion who pretends to be King? Take me to him. I will eat you later.' The rabbit led the lion to the edge of a large well. 'He's down there, master,' said Greybeard, 'resting in the cool water after his dinner. Look carefully and you will see him.'

The lion looked down and there in the water he saw a face just like his own. The lion roared and the echo came bellowing back. The lion swelled with anger and roared again, and the well trembled with its noise. 'How dare you challenge me!' roared the lion. 'I'll show you!' And still snarling with rage the lion leapt into the well. Splash! Down he sank in the water and was never seen again.

Old Greybeard looked into the well, and smiled at his own reflection in the water. Then he ran back to tell the other animals. The lion was dead, and they were free at last.

(Indian folktale)

The Lion who fell into a Hole

There was once a lion who did not look where he was going. One day he fell into a deep hole. The sides were steep and there was no way in which he could climb out. The lion roared for help.

A monkey heard the roar and peered down into the hole. 'Help me out of this hole,' said the lion.

'You ate one of my friends on Friday,' said the monkey. 'I am not going to help you!' And off went the monkey. Soon afterwards a zebra came by. The lion saw his stripes and shouted, 'Friend zebra! Get me out of this hole!'

'Oh no,' said the zebra. 'You are always chasing my friends and me. You stay in that hole and I'll feel safer!' The zebra galloped off, kicking up the dust as he went.

In a while a mouse came by. 'Dear mouse, help me out!' said the lion. The mouse peeped over the edge of the hole and twitched his whiskers. 'Oh no,' said the mouse. 'If I do you might eat my children.'

'If you let me out I promise that I will not eat your children,' said the lion. The mouse thought about it, then said, 'Very well, I will help you.' She saw a vine hanging from a nearby tree, so she took the end and dropped it down the hole. Slowly the lion climbed out. Then the lion pounced on the mouse and licked his lips. 'I promised not to eat your children, but I did not promise not to eat you!'

Just then, an owl who had been watching from the tree, flew down. He was determined to save the mouse. 'Lion, my dear friend,' said the owl. 'I heard that you were down the hole. How did you get out?' The lion, who was an honest animal, said, 'This mouse got me out.'

'I don't believe it,' hooted the owl. 'It is quite true,' said the lion. 'Show me how,' said the owl, 'and I will believe you.' The foolish lion jumped back into the hole. 'Now run away,' said the owl to the mouse, 'and be more careful who you help out of holes.'

(Indian folktale)

The Lost Sheep

There was once a shepherd who had a hundred sheep in his flock. He knew there were a hundred because he counted and loved each one of them. There were black sheep and white sheep, some very old sheep and some tiny baby lambs. It was a large flock to look after, but the shepherd was a kind and patient man.

Early in the morning he would lead his flock over the hills to find fresh grass for the sheep to feed on. All day the sheep grazed, drank from the stream or lay under the trees. There was nothing for them to fear for the shepherd kept good watch over them.

When evening came and the sun set over the hills the shepherd led them home again to the fold where they slept. As they passed through the gate the shepherd counted them to make sure that none was missing. Then he lit a fire outside the fold to frighten off any wild beasts who might be near. So day and night the shepherd tended his sheep.

One evening when black clouds covered the sky the shepherd led his flock home. The rain beat down and a cold wind blew. When he got to the fold he stood by the gate and counted the sheep in. 'One, two, three ...' and so on until 'ninety-seven, ninety-eight, ninety-nine.' That was the last sheep!

'There is one sheep missing,' thought the shepherd. 'If it is alone in the mountains all night it may die. I must find it.' So he lit a fire outside the fold, and set off again back towards the mountains. The night was dark and he felt tired. The rain poured down and the wind roared. He was cut by thorn bushes and brambles. Still he went on, calling for the lost sheep. He knew that there may be wild animals waiting in the darkness, and that the lost sheep would be cold and frightened. Sometimes he would stop to listen for the sound of a sheep. But no 'baa-a' came.

Then under a rocky ledge he saw something white. The shepherd scrambled over the rocks until he came to the lost sheep. Gently he lifted the sheep into his arms and covered it with his cloak. Then, very tired but very pleased, the shepherd carried the sheep home. He had found his lost sheep.

And that, said Jesus, is how God our Father cares for us.

The Magic Fish

Once upon a time an old fisherman caught a large fish that was all the colours of the rainbow and shone and sparkled in the water. The fish said, 'Oh please don't catch me because really I'm a prince,' and so the old fisherman let him go.

When he went back to his old hut that night the fisherman's wife said, 'Why haven't you caught any fish for supper?' And he told her, 'I did catch a fish but I let him go because he said he was a prince.' The wife was cross and said, 'You should not have let him go without asking for a wish. Go back at once.'

So the old fisherman went back to the seashore and called the fish and asked for a pretty house for his wife. When he returned the old hut was gone and in its place was a pretty house. For a while they were happy, then the cross old wife said, 'Go back to the sea and tell the fish I want to live in a castle.' Again the wish was granted and instead of a pretty house they had a grand castle to live in. For a while they were happy but then the cross old wife grew discontented again and ordered her husband to go back and ask the fish for another wish. 'Tell him,' she said, 'that I want to be queen.' The fisherman said, 'I don't want to go back again,' but his wife said, 'Go,' so he went.

The magic fish turned the fisherman's wife into a queen, and when the fisherman returned she was sitting on a golden throne wearing a golden dress and a golden crown, and for a while she was happy. Then she said, 'Go and tell the fish I want to be queen of the sun, moon and stars.' The fisherman groaned but again his cross old wife ordered him to go.

This time when the fisherman called to the fish from the seashore, and the fish appeared through the waves, shining and sparkling with his rainbow colours, the wish was not granted. 'Your wife has asked too much,' said the fish. 'I can't make her queen of the sun, moon and stars. And because she asks for too much, and always asks for more, now all your wishes will be taken away.'

So when the old fisherman returned home to his wife she was no longer queen in a castle, she was back in the old fisherman's hut, just like they were in the beginning, and that is where they had to stay.

(Chinese folktale)

The Man who said Thank You

One day as Jesus was walking down the street he heard some voices calling to him. 'Jesus! Jesus!' they called. 'Have pity on us. Please help us!'

Jesus stopped, and saw ten men sitting by the roadside. His friends stopped too, but they did not want to get near to these men. For each one of them had a terrible disease.

Jesus went over to where the men sat, and listened to what they had to say. They had nasty sores all over their bodies, and the illness had eaten away parts of their hands and their feet. Because of their disease the men were not allowed to live at home. They had to keep away from everyone. No one wanted them. So they were asking Jesus for help.

And Jesus said, 'You will be cured of your disease. Go to the priest and show him that you are really fit and healthy again.'

The men could hardly believe their ears. Slowly they got up and hobbled off on their poor lame feet. Then a wonderful thing happened. The sore places on their bodies became better. Their hands and feet grew strong and whole again. They began to laugh and shout, and ran off as fast as they could.

Suddenly one of them stopped. 'Wait,' he said to the other others. 'We have forgotten something. We never said "thank you" to Jesus.' But his friends were much too excited to listen. They wanted to show the priest that they were better, and then go home. So they would not wait.

The man turned round and ran back to Jesus. When he had caught Jesus up, he threw himself down and said, 'Thank you, Jesus. Thank you for curing me.' Jesus looked at the man and said, 'There were ten of you. Where are the other nine? You are the only one who remembered to say thank you.'

Then he put his hand on the man's shoulder and said, 'Get up now and go on your way. Your trust in me has made you well again.' And the man who had said thank you went on his way rejoicing.

The Man who sold his Shadow

There was once a young man named John who was always grumbling. He wanted above everything else to be rich and famous. One day his wish came true, and this is how it happened.

It was a hot sunny day and the sun was making long shadows everywhere. John was walking along the street when he was stopped by a merchant.

'You have a fine shadow there, young man,' said the merchant.

'Yes, my shadow always comes when the sun shines,' said John.

'I am buying shadows,' said the merchant. 'May I buy yours?'

'What will you give me for it?' asked John.

'If you give me your shadow I promise to make you rich and famous,' said the merchant. So John quickly agreed.

The merchant took a pair of scissors out of his pocket and bent down. Snip! Snip! He cut off John's shadow close at his heels, rolled it up and stuffed it into his bag. Then with a funny sort of laugh he raised his hat and walked away.

From that day on John's luck seemed to change. He became rich, and well known throughout the land. John became famous and his friends envied him. Then people began to notice something strange about John. 'Look!' they said. 'The sun is shining, yet John has got no shadow. How can that be?' They began to point at John whenever they saw him and whisper among themselves.

John began to notice how people avoided him, and stood staring at where his shadow should be. Poor John began to miss his shadow. He would jump quickly round to see if it was there. But no, even in the bright sunshine he had no shadow. John began to stay indoors when the sun was shining so people would not see him. Even when it was dull and cloudy he was frightened to go out in case he was seen. At last he was so miserable that he went to the merchant and begged to have his shadow back.

'All right,' said the merchant, 'but only if you give me all the riches you have gained.' John agreed, and he got his shadow back. And from that day on he never grumbled so much, for he knew that a happy life was made up of shadows as well as sunshine.

Mary and her Bones

Many years ago there was a girl called Mary Anning who lived in the seaside town of Lyme Regis in Dorset. She had no mother or father, and made her living by selling shells which she found by the seashore. She was good at collecting sea shells, and many that she found were very beautiful.

Each day Mary would climb over the rocks on the seashore with a basket in one hand and a hammer in the other. Here and there she would tap at a rock with her hammer, and look at the broken pieces very carefully to see if she could find a hidden shell. When she saw a shell she would put it in her basket, ready to sell to the holidaymakers who came to the town in summer.

One day Mary found something very strange in the rocks. It was a whole pattern of bones. It looked like a fish, but it was bigger than any fish Mary had ever seen. It was different, too, for it had flippers, instead of fins, on either side. So she asked some workmen to help her dig the rock out for her. A man named Mr Henley gave Mary £23 for the rock with the bones, which was a lot of money in those days. He said Mary had found something very important. The bones were the skeleton of a prehistoric monster, a kind of dinosaur called Ichthyosaurus, which means 'fish lizard'.

Mary found many other bones by the seashore. All were the bones of dinosaurs who had lived there millions of years ago. One of the skeletons she found was a 'flying lizard', called Pterodactyl. Although it had wings, it was not a bird. It had teeth and wings made of leathery skin. People came from all over the world to see the bones that Mary had found. She became famous, and you can see many of the skeletons she found in museums today.

When Mary died, a beautiful window was put in her local church at Lyme Regis to remind people of how she helped us to know more about prehistoric monsters.

The Mean Beggar

There was once a beggar who lived in a certain city. Each day he sat by the roadside holding out his hand to anyone who passed. His only possession was a begging bowl in which he kept his day's supply of rice.

One day a great Rajah came riding into the city on the back of his favourite elephant. The elephant stopped, knelt down, and the Rajah climbed down from his howdah (elephant seat). Behind him came a servant shielding him from the sun with an umbrella. By the roadside was the beggar, holding out his begging bowl.

'Please give me something,' he pleaded.

'No. Please give me something,' said the Rajah. The beggar shook his head, and the Rajah walked on.

Later that day the Rajah came back along the road. Once more the beggar was holding out his hand. 'Please give me something!' he cried.

'No. Please give me something,' replied the Rajah.

The beggar scratched his head. What did the poor beggar have that he could give to the rich Rajah? There was only his bowl of rice, and the beggar was looking forward to eating that. Carefully the beggar took from his bowl a single grain of rice, and handed it to the Rajah. 'Thank you,' said the Rajah. He took the grain of rice and popped it into his purse. Then from his purse he took something and placed it in the beggar's bowl. Then the Rajah went on his way.

The beggar couldn't wait to see what the Rajah had given him. When he looked into his bowl the beggar saw a tiny piece of gold, the size of one grain of rice. He gazed at it as it lay in the palm of his hand.

'I should have given him all my grains of rice,' he thought, 'for I received back only as much as I gave.'

(A legend from India)

The Milkmaid and her Pail

A milkmaid was walking to market one day. On her head she carried a large pail of milk. As she walked she began to think of all the money she would have when she sold the milk.

'With the money I shall buy some hens from Farmer Brown,' she thought. 'They will lay eggs for me every day. When the eggs hatch I will have at least a dozen chicks to sell at the market. With the money from the chicks I will buy myself a new dress.'

She continued to daydream as she walked along. 'I wonder what colour of dress I should buy?' she thought. 'Green, I think. That suits me best. A lovely green dress with a big frill at the hem. I will look so pretty that all the boys at the fair will want to dance with me. But I shall have nothing to do with them. I shall toss my head and walk away—just like this.'

With that she tossed her head. She had quite forgotten that she was carrying something on her head. Down fell the pail, spilling fresh, creamy milk all over the road.

'Oh, my milk!' she cried. 'Oh, my good fresh eggs! Oh, my little chicks! Oh, my beautiful green dress!'

It was too late. The milk had all trickled away among the stones of the street. Sadly the milkmaid brought her empty pail home to her mother. 'Ah, my daughter,' said her mother, 'you must remember—don't count your chickens before they are hatched.'

The Miller, the Son and the Donkey

One hot day a miller and his son were taking their donkey to market so they could sell him. They had not gone far along the road when they met some girls.

'How silly you are,' said one of the girls, 'walking to market. Why don't you ride on the donkey?'

So the miller sat his son on the donkey, and off they went, clip-clop-clip-clop, towards the town. After a while they met two old men. One old man said to the other, 'Look at that lazy boy riding while his poor father walks. Young people are so selfish these days!'

Hearing this, the miller's son jumped down and helped his father up on to the donkey's back. And off they went, clip-clop, towards the town. On their way they passed some women working in the fields. 'You cruel man,' said one of the women. 'Fancy riding on the donkey while your poor little son has to walk. Shame on you!'

So the miller, who was a kind-hearted man, picked up his son and placed the boy behind him on the donkey's back. As they drew near to the town they were stopped by a shepherd, who said, 'Tell me, is that your donkey?'

'Yes,' said the miller. 'Why do you ask?'

'Because that is no way to treat a donkey,' said the shepherd. 'Two of you on his back is much too heavy for the poor animal. You strong fellows are better able to carry the donkey than he is to carry you.'

So the miller and his son climbed down from the donkey's back. They tied the donkey's legs to a pole. They lifted the pole up and carried the donkey upside down between them. As they were crossing a bridge, the townspeople began to point and laugh at the strange sight of a donkey being carried on a pole. The noise so frightened the poor donkey that he began to kick and struggle. The miller and his son tried to keep hold of him, and they all fell with a splash into the river.

Sadly as they went home, dripping wet, the miller and his son decided that in future they would not do what everyone else said, but would think for themselves.

The Monkey and her Baby

The king of the gods once held a competition to find out which animal had the most beautiful baby. So one of every kind of animal came to show off their youngest child. All of them were keen to win the prize.

The animals paraded in a long line before the king. There was a cow and her baby calf, a dog and her puppy, a cat and her kitten, a sheep and her lamb, a lion and her cub, a goat and her kid—all the animals you can think of, with their babies, passed in front of the king. Having seen all the animals, the king of the gods was just about to announce the winner when an ugly monkey came hurrying in. She thrust her baby into the king's arms.

'Whatever is this?' asked the king, staring down at the little creature with its wrinkled face and screwed-up eyes. It was the ugliest thing the king had ever seen. He held the baby monkey well away from himself and stared at it. 'Take it away!' he said.

All the other animals began to laugh.

'I don't care what you say,' said the mother proudly, cuddling her baby in her arms. 'You can give the prize to anyone you like, but I know that my baby is the most beautiful of all.'

Monkeys, like all mothers, think that their own child is the best.

The Months of the Year

There was once a girl named Anna, who lived with her stepmother and sister on the edge of a great forest. Anna was a sweet and gentle girl but her stepmother and sister were very unkind to her. One cold January day her sister Greta said, 'Anna, go into the forest and fetch me some violets to wear.'

Greta knew that there were no violets to be found in winter-time. All day long Anna searched the forest for them. By evening she was feeling cold and hungry and a little frightened. Suddenly she saw a fire burning among the trees. She went closer and saw twelve strange creatures sitting on stone seats. They were the twelve Months of the Year.

'What do you want?' said January in a cold voice. Anna said she was looking for violets and that her sister would be cross if she returned without them. So the month of March rose and waved his wand over the fire. The flames leapt up and where there had been snow, violets were now growing. Anna picked a bunch, thanked the Months and ran home as fast as she could.

Her stepmother and sister were amazed to see the violets but did not even thank Anna. The next day Greta said, 'Go and pick me some strawberries.'

Again Anna went into the forest looking for strawberries on the snowy ground. Once more she saw the light of the fire, and the twelve Months. She told them what she was looking for and this time June waved the wand. At once ripe strawberries grew from the ground, and Anna was soon running home with them.

Her stepmother and sister were surprised; they ate the strawberries without giving Anna one of them. On the third day Greta said, 'Anna, go and fetch me some apples from the forest.' At once Anna went to where the twelve months sat, and asked for apples. September waved the wand and juicy red apples appeared on the trees. Happily Anna picked them and took them home.

'You should have brought more!' shouted Greta, who grabbed a bag and ran into the forest. She was looking for more apples to pick when she came to where the Months were sitting. 'What are you looking for?' asked January.

'Mind your own business!' said Greta rudely. As she looked up at the trees Greta did not notice as the Winter Months gathered round and waved the wand. At once the sky became dark and snow began to fall.

And Anna and her stepmother still wait for Greta to return.

Not True!

Once in a dark wood there lay a man's shoe. How it got there no one knew for no man had ever been near the wood. In fact the wild animals who lived there had never seen a man. But there it lay in the wood—a shoe.

The first to see it was the bear. He sniffed it and rolled it over with his great paws. He did not know what it was, so he called the other animals over to have a look. No one had ever seen a shoe before.

'I know what it is,' said the lion. 'It is the bark fallen off a tree.'

'Oh no,' said the leopard, 'it is the skin of a fruit.'

'I think it is the shell of a nut,' said the monkey.

'There's a hole for a bird,' said the wolf. 'It must be a bird's nest.'

'Look, here's a root,' said the goat, pulling at a shoelace. 'It is some kind of plant.'

Each animal thought he was right and they began to argue. The owl looked down as the animals got more and more angry with each other. 'If you all stop arguing I will tell you what it is,' said the owl. 'It is a man's shoe.'

'What?' cried the animals. 'What is a man? What is a shoe?'

'A man is an animal with two legs,' said the owl. 'He is like a bird, but he has no feathers. He can walk like us. He can eat like us, and he can talk like us. But he is much cleverer than us.'

'That can't be true,' growled the bear. 'How can an animal with two legs be cleverer than we who have four legs?'

'What I say is true,' said the owl. 'A man makes things like this to put on his feet. He calls them shoes.'

'Not true! Not true!' roared the lion. 'What animal would wear these on his feet?'

'Not true! Not true!' screeched the birds. 'How can there be an animal with two legs and no feathers?'

'Not true! Not true!' shouted all the animals. 'Who ever heard of such a thing?'

They were so angry with the poor old owl that they chased him out of the wood. 'Tu-whit-tuoo! But it is true!' said the owl. And of course it was.

(English folktale)

The Parts of the Body

A body is made up of many parts and they all work together. But it was not always so. Once, long ago, the parts of the body did not work well together at all. Each one had a will and a voice of its own.

It happened that the parts of the body began to find fault with the stomach. 'What does he do all day?' said the hands. 'We work hard for our living, but he's lazy, he just lies there while we give him things to eat.'

'Quite true,' said the feet. 'We have to walk miles carrying his great weight around.'

'What about us?' said the teeth. 'We are worn out with chewing food, just so that he can feel contented.'

'We've had enough,' said the hands. 'So have we,' stamped the feet. 'And us,' snapped the teeth. The other parts of the body agreed, and all decided that they would have nothing more to do with the stomach. The feet would not go to market, the hands would not carry food to the mouth, the mouth would not take food in, the teeth would not chew it—and so on for each part.

They had not been doing this for very long before they all began to feel very weak. The feet dragged slowly along the ground, the hands could hardly hold a pen, the teeth grew loose in the gums.

'You see how it is, my friends,' said the stomach. 'It is true that I cannot do anything without you. But how do you feel without me? The fact is that none of us can manage without the others. We only feel good if we work together.'

From that time on the parts of the body have worked together very well, but every now and then you will notice that the stomach has a grumble, just to let the body know that it has not forgotten the quarrel completely.

The Rich Man's Diamond

Once upon a time there lived a very rich man. But although he had so much money he was a very selfish man. He never gave presents to anyone, nor did he help the many poor people in town who had no money to buy food. 'If they have got no food, they will have to starve,' he said to himself.

One day this rich man visited a fortune teller. The rich man wanted to know how much money he was going to make in the coming year. 'I shall look into my crystal ball,' said the fortune teller, 'and tell you what will happen.' The fortune teller gazed into his crystal ball, and said, 'What a kind and generous man you are. I see that all your money is going to be given to the poor.'

The rich merchant could hardly believe his ears. He had never given anything away in his life. The very idea of it made him feel ill. He began to think how he could keep all his money with him so that no poor person would ever get his hands on it. Then he had an idea.

He took all his money to a jeweller's and bought a great big diamond. Then he carefully sewed the diamond inside the lining of his hat. No one would know it was there, and he could keep it with him always. Soon after, the rich man decided to go on holiday and sail by ship to another country. So he packed his bag, and with his hat firmly on his head he went on board the boat.

The ship had not been at sea for long when a great storm blew up. The winds blew the ship on to some rocks, and it sank beneath great waves. The rich man's hat was washed overboard, and slowly it sank into the sea and disappeared. When the storm was over nothing could be seen of the ship, the rich man's hat or his diamond.

Back in the town later that day a poor man bought his family their only food for that day—a large wet fish, which a fishing boat had just brought in. As the family gathered round the table the man cut the fish open and what did he see—a large glittering diamond!

The family sold the rich man's diamond for a great sum of money, but instead of keeping it all for themselves, they shared it among the poor people of the town. So the fortune teller's words came true—the money of the rich man had after all been given to the poor.

St Francis and the Wolf

There was once a good man named St Francis who was so kind to everyone that even the birds and animals loved him.

One day St Francis came to a town where everyone was frightened. They were scared to leave their houses for there was a fierce wolf living in the forest nearby. This wolf attacked and killed anyone that it could find. As St Francis came along the men of the town armed with sticks were going out to hunt the wolf and to kill it.

'Let me go and speak to Brother Wolf,' said St Francis.

'If you go near him he will kill you,' said the men. But St Francis was not afraid. Alone and unarmed he set off for the forest where the wolf lived. As he came near the wolf's den, he heard a growl and saw a grey shape between the trees. Then the wolf sprang out baring its sharp teeth. St Francis stood quite still and spoke gently to it. When the wolf heard his voice it became quiet.

'Come here, Brother Wolf,' he called. 'Do not harm me.' At once the wolf came up to St Francis and lay down by his feet. Then he told the wolf how wrong it was to hurt and to frighten the poor people of the town. 'Come with me back to the town,' said St Francis, 'and show the people that you are sorry. They they will feed you.' Then St Francis returned to the town and the wolf followed him like a dog.

The people were amazed to see St Francis walking along with the wolf. But when they saw how gentle the wolf had become they fed it, and even let it walk in and out of their houses. The wolf did no one any harm and became a friend to everyone in the town. They called it 'Brother Wolf', and remembered the time when St Francis had made the wild wolf his friend.

St Jerome and the Lion

Long ago there lived a good man called St Jerome. He lived with his friends in a big house called a monastery. One day as he sat by the gate of the monastery he suddenly saw a lion coming towards him. His friends ran for safety but Jerome sat and waited. He could see that the lion had hurt himself.

The lion was limping and Jerome could see blood dripping from his paw. There was a huge thorn sticking into it. Gently Jerome pulled it out and bathed the lion's injured paw. Then instead of going away the lion lay down at Jerome's feet as if to say, 'I am going to stay here with you.'

The lion stayed with Jerome and followed him everywhere. So to give him a job Jerome told him to guard the donkey that lived with them in the monastery. But one day while the donkey was in the meadow eating grass the lion yawned and fell fast asleep. When he awoke the donkey was gone. Robbers had stolen him while the lion lay asleep. When Jerome's friends heard that the donkey was gone they said the lion must have eaten the donkey. 'From now on,' said Jerome, 'the lion will have to do the donkey's work.'

So the lion had to pull the carts and carry the wood just as the donkey had done. Then one day the lion saw a lot of merchants with camels carrying many fine things on their way to market. In front of the camels was an old man leading a donkey. Suddenly the lion lifted his head and sniffed the air. Then with a glad roar he jumped forward, for he had recognised his donkey friend. When the merchants saw the lion they ran for their lives. But the lion chased after them and drove them all—merchants, camels and donkey— back to the monastery.

Jerome and his friends were pleased to see the lion and the donkey together again. The merchants admitted that it was they who had stolen the donkey. 'Please forgive us,' they begged. Because he had a kind heart Jerome forgave them and told them to go in peace.

So the lion stayed till the end of his days with the donkey, and with the man who had cared for him—St Jerome.

St Nicholas and the Gifts

Many years ago there lived a good man named St Nicholas. In the town where he lived there were many poor people. Some of them were so poor that they even had to sell their own children to get enough to eat.

In the town there lived a poor man who had three daughters. One night as St Nicholas passed the poor man's cottage he heard the sound of crying. He stopped and listened. A girl's voice was saying, 'Father, let us go into the streets to beg for food. Please do not sell us.' Then Nicholas heard the father say, 'Well, we will wait for just one more night, and pray that someone will help us.'

When Nicholas heard this he hurried home, for he knew that in his treasure chest he had three bags of gold. That night when everyone was fast asleep he returned to the cottage. It was a cold snowy night but there was one window left open. Nicholas dropped a bag of gold coins through the opening and hurried away.

The next morning the man was amazed to find the bag of gold. It was enough to save his eldest daughter from being sold. The man had no idea where the gold had come from and so thanked God for his gift.

The next night Nicholas came again to the cottage and dropped a bag of gold in for the second daughter. Then secretly he hurried away. On the third night the man made up his mind to keep watch, so he crept out and hid himself near the cottage. When it was dark he heard the sounds of footsteps, and saw St Nicholas dropping his third bag of gold through the cottage window. The poor man then rushed out from where he was hiding to thank St Nicholas.

'Please tell no one, not even your daughters,' said St Nicholas. 'It is just my way of making others happy.'

But people came to hear of this and many other gifts of kindness that St Nicholas did. In Holland he became the favourite saint of children, who called him Santa Claus. And today all over the world children hang up their stockings in the hope that Santa Claus will give them presents on Christmas Eve.

St Valentine and the Blind Girl

Many years ago in the city of Rome there lived a little girl who was blind. There were many beautiful buildings and sunny streets in the city but the little girl could not see them. She had never seen her mother or father and only knew they were there by the sound of their voices. But one day her life was changed, and this is how it happened.

The little girl's father worked for the Roman Emperor who was the king of the city. The Emperor in those days hated people who were Christians and whenever he caught them he would lock them up in prison. One day the Emperor told the girl's father that he must keep a prisoner in his house. 'Take this man Valentine,' said the Emperor, 'and lock him up in your house. He is a Christian and will not stop talking about Jesus Christ.' So the girl's father took Valentine back to his house.

The little girl was waiting for her father, and listening for the sound of his footsteps. When he came she kissed him and said, 'Who is that with you, father?' Then Valentine said, 'Bless this house and help everyone to know that Jesus is the Light of the World.'

The little girl had never heard the name of Jesus before and said, 'Why do you say that Jesus is the light of all the world?' Valentine then began to tell the girl about how Jesus healed the sick and brought happiness to the people who believed in him. Then the girl's father said, 'If Jesus is the light of the world as you say, see if he can cure my daughter of her blindness.'

So Valentine said, 'Come here, my child.' The little girl stretched out her hands to feel her way towards him. She then heard the voice of Valentine say, 'Lord Jesus, who is the Light of the World, give your light to this little child.' Valentine then put his hands on her eyes and opened them. For the first time the little girl could see. She looked at the sunshine, the blue sky and the house where they lived. She saw her father and her mother, and bright colours all round her. All that was dark was light, now that she could see.

Everyone in the house rejoiced at the good news and became Christians, like Valentine, and followers of Jesus.

The Shirt of Happiness

There was once a very grumpy king. Nothing ever seemed to go right for him. He grumbled when he got up in the morning; it was either too early or too late. He moaned about his food; there was either too much or too little. He found something wrong with everything. When he was not complaining he was worrying. He was a very unhappy king.

One day he called all his ministers together and asked if they could help him. 'I feel so unhappy,' said the king. 'Can any of you suggest a solution to my problem?' The ministers all shook their heads, then the oldest one spoke. 'Your majesty,' he said, 'there is only one way to cure your problem. You must find the Shirt of Happiness and wear it. No one knows what the shirt looks like, only that it belongs to a truly happy man.'

'Very well,' said the king. 'Each of you must search my kingdom until you find this truly happy man. When you have found him, bring me his shirt so that I can wear it.' So the ministers went off to search for the Shirt of Happiness. But nowhere , in the countryside or the town, could they find a truly happy man. At last they found one truly happy man, but he was so poor that he did not have a shirt. So what were the ministers to say to the king? The oldest minister had an idea.

The king called the ministers to the palace and asked if anyone had found the Shirt of Happiness. 'Yes,' said the minister. 'Here it is.' Then he handed the king an old but rather fine-looking white shirt. The king tried it on at once, and it fitted perfectly. The ministers all smiled, and the king smiled back at them. The king felt happy and wore his special shirt every day. Never had he felt better or enjoyed himself more. The Shirt of Happiness really seemed to work.

A few days later he noticed that one of his old shirts was missing from the royal wardrobe. You wouldn't think that now he had his Shirt of Happiness he would mind missing one of his old shirts. But it set him thinking, and he sent for his old minister. The old minister then confessed the whole story; so as not to disappoint the king he had taken one of the king's own shirts and pretended it was the Shirt of Happiness. At first the king was very angry, but then he laughed. That old shirt had taught him a lesson—it was much more fun being happy than unhappy.

'From today,' said the king, 'I shall make all my shirts Shirts of Happiness.'

Solomon and the Baby

In far-off days, so the Bible tells us, there was a king named Solomon. Everyone loved Solomon for he was a good and wise king. Whenever they had any troubles the people knew that Solomon would always listen and try to help them. Each morning he would sit on a great throne in his court and wait to see who would come to ask for his help.

One day a great noise was heard as two women came into court arguing at the tops of their voices. 'Silence in court!' said the Captain of the Guard. The women stopped arguing. 'Now tell me,' said Solomon, 'what is wrong ... one at a time, please!'

'Great king,' said one of the women, 'you must decide between this woman and myself. We both live in the same house and a little while ago each of us had a baby. One night this woman's baby died. She was very sad and then she did a terrible thing. At night while I was asleep she crept into my room and stole my baby. She says that it is my baby that died, and the live baby is hers. I cannot prove the baby is mine, but it is.'

Then the other woman spoke. 'The baby is mine. What this woman says about one baby dying is true, but the baby who died was hers. Now she has no baby, and she wants to take mine.'

Solomon looked at the two women and then said, 'Bring the baby here.' In a few minutes the tiny baby was brought in and placed in front of Solomon. 'As you both say the baby is yours I have decided that the baby shall be cut in two, and that each mother shall have half the baby. It is the only fair thing to do, don't you agree?'

Solomon then took out his sword, raised it high above his head, and waited.

'O wise king,' said the first woman, 'whatever you say is right.'

'No, no!' shouted the second woman. 'Please don't kill the baby! Let her have him. I'd rather the baby were hers than killed.'

Solomon smiled, lowered his sword and said to her, 'You are the true mother of the child, for no real mother who loved her baby would want to see him killed.' Solomon handed the baby to the true mother who took the child happily into her arms. Once more Solomon had shown that he was a good and wise king.

The Timid Hares

There was once a timid hare who was always afraid that something terrible was going to happen. He was always saying, 'What if the earth were suddenly to fall in? Whatever would happen to me then?'

One day after he had been saying this to himself many times, a large coconut fell from a tree. Bang! The hare jumped as if he had been shot. 'What was that?' he cried. 'The earth must be falling in!' So he ran off as fast as he could go. After a while he met another hare. 'Brother hare,' he said, 'run for your life! The earth is falling in!'

'What was that?' cried the other hare. 'Hey, wait for me!' So he ran after the first hare, who told another hare, and soon all the hares were running as fast as they could. And each one cried, 'Run, run, the earth is falling in, the earth is falling in!'

Soon the larger animals heard and they too began to run, crying, 'The earth is falling in! Run for your lives!' A wise old lion saw them running and heard their cries. He looked around. 'I cannot see the earth falling in,' he said. So in his loudest voice he roared, 'Stop!' At this all the frightened animals skidded to a halt. Quickly they told him that the earth was falling in.

'What makes you think so?' asked the lion.

'The tigers told us,' trumpeted the elephants. 'The bears told us,' growled the tigers. 'The buffaloes told us,' grunted the bears. 'The monkeys told us,' bellowed the buffaloes. 'The jackals said so,' chattered the monkeys. 'The hares told us,' yelped the jackals. One hare said that another had told him and so on until finally they came to the first hare. 'I know because I saw it happen,' said the hare. 'Under the big coconut tree.'

'Well, climb up on my back and show me,' said the lion. So the hare jumped up, still trembling, on the lion's back, and slowly they plodded to the big tree. Just then—Bang! Another coconut came crashing to the ground.

'Run, run,' cried the timid hare. 'We are all going to be killed!'

'Stop and look,' said the lion. 'It's only a coconut falling from the palm tree.' The animals all laughed when they heard, and the timid hare realised what a fool he had been.

The Town Mouse and the Country Mouse

Once upon a time the Country Mouse invited his cousin the Town Mouse to stay with him.

The Country Mouse lived alone under a hedge in the corner of a field. The Country Mouse did not have fine food but he was happy to share what he had with the Town Mouse. There were grains of wheat and barley, nuts and some stale cheese. The Town Mouse did not think much of this country food. He nibbled a bit and then turned up his nose.

'Dear Cousin,' he said, 'how can you eat such plain food? Come and visit me in the city. I'll give you a good dinner. Besides, life in the country is so dull. Nothing ever seems to happen. There is always a lot going on in the town, and food is just left lying around for you to eat.'

So the Country Mouse agreed to go back with the Town Mouse to the big city where he lived. By the time they arrived at the Town Mouse's home it was dark. They went in through a hole in the wall. The Town Mouse led the Country Mouse right into a grand dining room. On the table were the leftovers of a fine feast, with foods of every kind.

'Is this food all for us?' asked the Country Mouse.

'Of course. Didn't I tell you?' said the Town Mouse. 'Help yourself.' So the two mice climbed on to the table and were soon eating jam and cake, cheese and trifle and many other tasty titbits. Suddenly the door of the room flew open and a crowd of laughing noisy people came in to finish off the feast. The two mice jumped off the table in fright and hid themselves behind a curtain.

After a long time the room grew quiet again, and the mice came out and climbed back on to the table. Then something even more frightening happened. 'Listen! What is that?' said the Country Mouse. There was not a sound but they could see something creeping towards them. 'It's a cat! Run for your life,' said the Town Mouse. The two mice managed to run into the hole just in time.

The Country Mouse made up his mind to go back to the country that very night. 'What! Going so soon?' said the Town Mouse. 'I would rather eat my plain food in peace than run these risks for my dinner,' said the Country Mouse. And he ran back as fast as he could to his comfortable country life.

Why the Bat flies at Night

Bats are stange animals. They have bodies like mice but they can fly in the air like birds. They live in dark places, and only come out at night. This is a story that tells you why.

There was once a war between the birds and four-footed animals. The bat was not sure which side to join. He wanted to be on the winning side. He thought he would wait and see what happened.

At first the birds were winning the war, so the bat joined the birds. He said he was one of them. In one way he was like a bird—he could fly. Before long the animals won a big battle. 'Oh dear,' thought the bat. 'I have chosen the losing side.' Quickly he changed sides. 'I am no bird,' he said. 'I have no feathers. I cannot sing. I shall join my four-footed friends.'

The bat was very useful to the four-footed animals because he could fly and was able to attack the birds in the air. But the birds grew stronger and won the war after all. The bat still wanted to be on the winning side so he went back to the birds.

'Oh no,' said the birds. 'You cannot join us. When we were losing the war you left us. You are no friend of ours. Go back to the four-footed animals.' When the bat went back to the animals, they did not want him. 'Oh no,' they said. 'You cannot join us. You only came to us because the birds would not have you. You are no friend of ours, we do not want you. Go away.'

So the bat went off alone to live in a cave. None of the birds nor four-footed animals wanted the bat near them. Ever since that time the bat has not wanted to come out in the daylight. Even today he flies by night so that no one can see him.

Why the Robin has a Red Breast

Here is a story told by the Red Indian people about how they made their first fire.

Many years ago the Red Indians had no fire. Only one fire burned in their lands. This was kept in a wigwam and guarded by three witches. The three witches were mean and selfish; they wanted the fire all to themselves, and would allow no one to take even the smallest of the burning branches. In winter the Red Indians suffered terribly when the cold winds blew and the snows began to fall.

One day the Red Indian chief called all his braves together. 'Brother braves, we must have fire,' he said. 'Who will fetch it for us from the witches?' None of the braves answered him. 'If there is no one brave enough, perhaps our animal friends will help us. I have a plan,' said the chief. 'Now listen carefully.'

The braves listened, and agreed to help the chief with his plan. This is what happened. The next day the three witches were crouching over their fire when they heard a knock on the door of their wigwam. It was a wolf. 'Please let me warm myself by your fire,' said the wolf, 'for my old bones are frozen.'

'All right,' growled the witch, 'but not for long.'

The wolf sat by the fire and gave a thundering great sneeze.

'Aa-tish-oo!' It was a signal. Outside the Indians shouted their war cries. The witches rushed out, thinking they were being attacked. Quickly the wolf seized a burning branch and ran outside. He then threw it to the deer who raced into the woods. At once the witches jumped on to their broomsticks and went chasing after him. Just as they were about to catch the deer he threw the flaming stick to the robin. The robin in those days was a dull brown bird. With the branch in his beak he flew off, followed by the witches. The fire was hot and burned a bright red patch on his chest. But he flew his fastest and finally gave the burning stick to an Indian brave. With it he lit a great fire which frightened off the witches.

The chief's plan had worked. The Indians had fire, and the robin had a red breast.

Why the Spider lives in a Web

There was a time when all the animals liked the Spider. But the Spider's special friends were Tiger and Monkey. This was funny, for they were big and Spider was small; they liked work and Spider did not; they did not steal but Spider did.

Tiger and Monkey had three fields. They grew yams in one field, potatoes in another, and corn in the third. Spider used to sit and watch while they worked. When the yams were ready to be dug up, Tiger and Monkey went to dig them and found that some had been taken. So they set a trap. The next day they went to the field they saw someone in the trap—it was Spider!

'Please let me go,' said Spider. 'I will never come here again.' So they let him go. When the potatoes were ready for digging, Tiger and Monkey took their forks into the field. But they found that some of their potatoes were missing. So Monkey said he would keep watch that night and try to catch the thief. Sure enough as Monkey sat in the dark he saw someone digging the potatoes. Monkey crept down, ran across the field and caught hold of— Spider.

'Oh, please let me go,' said Spider. 'I will never steal again.' This time they beat him and let him go. Then Tiger and Monkey went into their third field to cut the corn. But somebody had been there before them for there was some corn missing. Tiger and Monkey guessed who it was, and kept watch for Spider. The next night Spider went into the field of corn. Tiger and Monkey crept after him. Spider did not know they were there, and happily began cutting and eating the corn. Then he turned round, and there were Tiger and Monkey.

Spider ran as fast as he could and after him ran Tiger and Monkey. The chase was fast and furious through the forest. As he rushed past a banana tree Spider tore off a thin, strong thread. Then he raced up to an orange tree and tied an end round one of the branches. From this he swung to another tree and the thread made a bridge. When Tiger climbed one tree Spider ran to the other. When Monkey climbed that tree Spider ran to the middle of his bridge and sat there.

Spider was safe. But what could he eat, hanging high on his thread? Spider was a clever fellow, so he found out how to spin a web to catch flies to eat. And he has been doing the same thing ever since.

(West Indian folktale)

The Young Man and the Swallow

There was once a young man who was left a large fortune when his father died. Instead of looking after the money carefully he spent it as fast as he could and soon it was all gone.

All that the young man had left of any value were his warm winter clothes. He had a long coat made of the finest fur, some fur-lined gloves and a pair of fur-lined leather boots. It had been a cold winter, but the young man had kept warm in his thick fur clothes.

One day in early spring he looked out of his bedroom window and saw a swallow flying under the roof of his house. 'If a swallow is here it must be a sign that summer has come,' said the young man. 'Now I can sell my winter clothes and make some money again.'

So he ran out to the shops and sold his fine fur coat, his fur-lined gloves and his fur-lined leather boots. The furs were valuable and the shopkeeper gave him a good price for them. But the young man had not changed. He went straight out and spent all the money enjoying himself at the fair. By evening he had nothing left.

The next day when the young man woke up he was shivering with cold. The weather had changed in the night. The north wind blew, and there had been a hard frost. There was snow on the ground and the young man had no warm clothes to wear—only a thin shirt and an old pair of trousers. He peered through his bedroom window and there on the windowsill lay the swallow. Yesterday it had been building its nest in the sunshine. Today it was now half-dead with cold.

'Poor thing,' said the young man. 'I thought you had brought the summer with you. I should have known that one swallow does not make a summer.'

Prayers

1.   Father, we thank you for the night,
     And for the pleasant morning light;
     For rest and food and loving care
     And all that makes the day so fair.

     Help us to do the things we should,
     To be to others kind and good;
     In all we do at work or play
     To grow more loving every day.

2.   Thank you for the world so sweet,
     Thank you for the food we eat;
     Thank you for the birds that sing,
     Thank you, God, for everything.

3.   Dear Lord Jesus, we shall have this day only once; before it is gone,
     help us to do all the good we can, so that today is not a wasted day.
                              Stephen Grellet (1773–1855)

4.   God bless all our cities
     Each road, street and square,
     God look down on every house
     And bless the people there.

5.   Loving Father, we praise you for the wonderful things which you
     have given us:
              For the beautiful sun
              For the rain which makes things grow
              For the woods and the fields
              For the sea and the sky
              For the flowers and the birds
              And for all your gifts to us.
              Everything around us rejoices.
              Help us also to rejoice and give us thankful hearts.

6. **The Knight's Prayer**
God be in my head
 And in my understanding.
God be in my eyes
 And in my looking.
God be in my mouth
 And in my speaking.
God be in my heart
 And in my thinking.
God be at my end
 And at my departing.
from *The Book of Hours* (1514)

7. Jesus, may I be like you,
 Loving, kind, in all I do,
 Kind and happy when I play
 Close beside you all the day.

8. O God, thank you for making us happy at home and at school. Help us to make other people happy for the sake of our Lord Jesus Christ.

9. Little drops of water
  Little grains of sand
 Make a mighty ocean
  And a pleasant land.

 Little deeds of kindness
  Little words of love,
 Make this earth an Eden
  Like the heaven above.
    Isaac Watts

10. Heavenly Father, please forgive me
 For the things I have done wrong
 For bad temper and angry words
 For the times I am selfish and greedy
 For the times I have made others unhappy
 Forgive me, heavenly Father.

11. Dear Lord give us the courage to own up when we have done things wrong, so that we may be forgiven, as you forgive those who are truly sorry.

12. Dear Jesus, help us to forgive those who have been unkind to us, just as you forgave those who hurt you.

13. Dear God, thank you for our pets, for friendly dogs and cats and rabbits, for guinea pigs and goldfish and for all the animals who share our lives. Help us to care for them as you care for us.

14. Dear Father,
Thank you for all creatures small
For crawling beasts and singing birds
For animals both large and tall
Hear our words and bless them all.

15. Bless, O Lord, the animals of the farm
the cows who give us meat and milk
the sheep who give us wool
chickens who lay us eggs to eat
horses, turkeys, ducks and geese,
take good care of them all.

16. Day by Day, dear Lord, of thee three things I pray,
To see thee more clearly,
Love thee more dearly,
Follow thee more nearly,
Day by day.
Richard of Chichester (1197–1253)

17. Dear Lord Jesus, we pray for those who are unhappy today
    for those who have no food to eat
    for those without homes or families
    for those who are sick or frightened
    for those who are alone
    and have no people to love them.

18. The Lord is my shepherd,
    I have everything I need,
    He lets me rest in fields of green grass
    and leads me to quiet pools of fresh water.
    He gives me new strength.

    He guides me in the right way,
    as he has promised.
    Even if I go through the deepest darkness
    I will not be afraid, Lord
    because you are with me.

    from *Psalm* 23

19. Dear Father of our world family, love and care for children everywhere. Make them happy, keep them safe from danger, and help them to grow up strong and good.

20. Heavenly Father help us to love one another, and to play our part in bringing peace and happiness to the world.

21. Dear God, thank you for being there
    When I wake up in the morning
    When I come to school each day
    When I play with my friends
    And when I go to bed at night,
    Thank you God for being there.

22. Dear God sometimes we are scared by the things that we see and hear. Help us to remember that we need never be afraid for we have you, our Father, to care for us and watch over us.

23. Let us with a gladsome mind
    Praise the Lord for he is kind.
                John Milton

24. Thank you God for this new day,
    For fun and friends, at work and play,
    Thank you for your loving care
    At home, at school and everywhere.

25. God bless all those that I love. And God bless those that love me.

26. Dear God help to make the people of the world one family, and help us to love our brothers and sisters all over the world.

27. Dear Lord bless all growing things and help me to grow in goodness and love.

28. Dear Lord, open my eyes to see what is beautiful, my mind to know what is true and my heart to love what is good.

29. Jesus, friend of little children,
    Be a friend to me,
    Take my hand and ever keep me
    Close to thee.

30. Two little eyes to look to God,
    Two little ears to hear his word,
    Two little feet to walk in his ways,
    Two little lips to sing his praise,
    Two little hands to do his will
    And one little heart to love him still.

31. Dear God thank you for holidays
    For sunshine and for fresh air
    For seaside and open spaces
    For the fun and games we share
    And for the chance to see other places
    We thank you God.

32. Dear God bless all the people on the roads today,
    bless the people driving cars, buses and lorries,
    bless the people riding bicycles and scooters,
    bless the people walking along streets and busy roads,
    please help them to be careful on the roads today
    and help us to take care when we cross the roads.

33. Help us good Lord to be thankful for the gifts we have received from
    you and help us to share those gifts with others who are in need.

34. The things, good Lord, that we pray for,
    give us grace to work for.
                              Sir Thomas More

35. Dear Jesus bless my hands today
    And may the things they do
    Be kind, loving and helpful
    Two busy hands for you.

36. O Lord, bless our school, that working together and playing
    together, we may learn to serve you and to serve one another.

37. Dear God, be good to me, the sea is so wide and my boat is so small.
                              Prayer of the Breton fishermen

38.   Dear God thank you for sending rain to make the flowers and trees grow. For sending rain that we may have water to drink and rain to make puddles to splash in.

39.   All good gifts around us,
      Are sent from heaven above,
      Then thank the Lord, O thank the Lord,
      For all his love.

40.   Bread is a lovely thing to eat—
      God bless the barley and the wheat.
      A lovely thing to breathe is air—
      God bless the sunshine everywhere.
      The earth's a lovely place to know—
      God bless the folks that come and go!
      Alive's a lovely thing to be—
      Giver of life—we say—bless thee!

41.   Dear Lord Jesus please help us to remember that it is better to give things than to get them. Help us to give to others, to give our help at home, to give our best work at school, and to give turns to others when we play.

42.   Be near me, Lord Jesus, I ask thee to stay
      Close by me forever, and love me, I pray.
      Bless all the dear children in thy tender care;
      And fit us for heaven to live with thee there.
                                            Martin Luther.

43.   Lord of the loving heart, may mine be loving too.
      Lord of the gentle hands, may mine be gentle too.
      Lord of the willing feet, may mine be willing too.
      So I may grow more like you
      In all I say and do.

44. Heavenly Father, we think today of children all over the world. Help us to remember that people from every land belong to one big family of brothers and sisters. May we live together in peace and friendship, loving you and loving one another.

45. God bless the field and bless the furrow,
Stream and branch and rabbit burrow,
Bless the sun and bless the sleet,
Bless the lane and bless the street.
Bless the minnow, bless the whale,
Bless the rainbow and the hail,
Bless the nest and bless the leaf,
Bless the good man and the thief,
Bless the wing and bless the fin,
Bless the air I travel in.
Bless the earth and bless the sea,
God bless you and God bless me!
                adapted from *The Robin's Song*,
                an old English rhyme.

46. Do all the good you can
By all the means you can
In all the ways you can
In all the places you can
At all the times you can
To all the people you can
As long as ever you can.
                John Wesley

47. Thank you God, for the fun of bonfires and fireworks, and for the warmth of fires on cold nights.

48. Dear God, give me helping hands and a loving heart.

49. Wherever I go by night or day,
    I know I'm safe along the way,
    Because the Lord is there.
    On the land or on the sea,
    I know that God is there with me,
    For God is everywhere.

50. Dear God, sometimes I am not sure which way to go. Thank you for signposts which show me the way and thank you for people who show me the way when I feel lost, lonely or frightened.

51. The moon shines bright
    And the stars give light
    Before the break of day.
    God bless you all
    Both great and small
    And send you a joyful day.

52. We thank you loving Father
    For all your tender care
    For food and clothes and shelter
    And all the world so fair.

53. God, our great Creator gave to us these summer days. Let us thank him
        for the fun of playing in the open air
        for our games, picnics and outings
        for singing birds, green trees and sweet flowers
        for all that we enjoy in the long summer days
    We offer now our thanks and praise.

54. Thank you God for this wonderful world. For the great creatures that lived long ago. For wild animals that live in far-off lands. For small creatures in gardens, fields and woods, And for the pets who share our homes.
    We thank you God.

55. Dear Lord, help us to make the world a cleaner and tidier place by not leaving any litter in our homes, streets or school.

56. Dear Lord, thank you for our eyes with which we see the beautiful colours of flowers, pictures, animals and people. Open our eyes to the beauty of our world.

57. Dear God, thank you for all the interesting and new things we are learning to do at home and at school each day.

58. Thank you God for the joys of Christmas. For the fun of parties and presents. For Christmas trees and pretty lights. For carols, and the songs we sing and for all the happiness of Christmas time. Thank you most of all that Jesus was born as a baby on the first Christmas Day.

59. Light the candles on the tree,
     Christ was born for you and me.
     Light the candles in the hall,
     He was born to help us all.
     Light the candles up and down,
     In the country and the town.
     Light the candles everywhere,
     He was born a baby fair.
                    Christina Rossetti.

60. We thank you Heavenly Father for the joys of winter, for the beauty of frost and falling snow, for warm clothes and cosy fires and the shelter of our homes on stormy nights. We thank you for this time when seeds are safely asleep in the earth ready to wake again in the warm days of spring.

61.   For flowers that bloom about our feet;
       For tender grass, so fresh, so sweet;
       For song of bird, and hum of bee;
       For all things fair we hear or see,
       Father in Heaven, we thank thee!

       For blue of stream and blue of sky;
       For pleasant shade of branches high;
       For fragrant air and cooling breeze;
       For beauty of the blooming trees,
       Father in Heaven, we thank thee!
                       R. Emerson

62.   Dear God, when we are sad or find it hard to do what is right help us to remember Jesus who died for us on the cross and came alive again on Easter Day.

63.   **A Prayer for Special Days**
       God, our loving Father hear us
       Bless us on this special day
       May we know that you are with us
       Keep us safe in every way.

       May we learn to help each other
       Love and care for everyone
       Hear us as we pray together
       As in heaven, Your will be done.

64.   To God our Father now we bring,
       Our prayers and songs of praise,
       To God who gives us everything,
       Our thanks for Autumn days.

65. All things bright and beautiful,
    All creatures great and small,
    All things wise and wonderful,
    The Lord God made them all.

    Each little flower that opens,
    Each little bird that sings,
    He made their glowing colours,
    He made their tiny wings.

    The cold wind in the winter,
    The pleasant summer sun,
    The ripe fruits in the garden—
    He made them every one.

    He gave us eyes to see them,
    And lips that we might tell,
    How great is God Almighty,
    Who has made all things well.
                        Mrs Alexander

66. For all the foods we like to eat,
    For milk and eggs and fish and meat,
    For juicy fruits both green and red,
    For golden corn to make our bread,
    We thank you Father for this food,
    Which makes us strong and does us good.

67. Dear God, thank you for all those people who help us day by day
    especially for our ... (mothers/fathers/teachers/policemen/
    firemen/farmers, etc)
    We thank you Father for their care,
    For all your children everywhere.

68. Thank you God for the treasures of the earth; for the trees and plants that grow in the earth; for the animals that make their homes in the earth; for the coal, oil and precious stones that we dig from the earth.
Thank you God for all the good things that we get from the earth.

69. This is our school
Let peace dwell here
Let the room be full of contentment
Let love be here
Love of one another
Love of mankind
And love of God.
Let us remember
That as many hands build a house
So many hearts make a school.

70. Now may God bless us and keep us; may he give us light to guide us; courage to support us; and love to unite us; this day and for evermore. Amen.

Resources

A Checklist of Resources

Resource Books
1. Story Books
2. Poetry Books
3. Song Books
4. Miscellanies of stories, poems and songs
5. Assembly Books

A Checklist of Resources

Some of the resources available to add variety to the presentation of meetings or assemblies with young children.

Art work—painting, drawing, patterns, printing, models, etc.
Bible stories—plays and pictures.
Children's writing—news, descriptions, stories, poems, plays, etc.
Collections—display and discuss collected items of a child or group of children.
Cooking—menus, recipes, kitchen equipment, ingredients, tasting!
Crafts—collage, constructions, origami, mobiles, tie-and-dye, etc.
Dance—music and movement, folk dances, ballet, disco, etc.
Drama—mime and dressing-up, plays and make-believe.
Experiments in science and nature study.
Explanations of magic tricks and how things work.
Festivals—religious, national, international, local, school, etc.
Films, filmstrips, overhead projector or slides.
Music to listen to, music for movement, musical instruments (played and/or made)
News—international, national, local, school and home events.
Number games, songs, rhymes and puzzles.
Nursery rhymes—origins, meanings and adaptations in song, movement and mime.
Objects of interest, natural or man-made, found or created.
Pictures, prints, posters, charts or projected image.
Poems—read, recited (solo or choral speaking) acted or made up.
Projects—displays, books, children's work, ideas and research.
Puppets—finger, hand, marionettes, masks, etc., used to illustrate stories.
Questions, quizzes, riddles, tongue-twisters, jokes and word-play.
Songs, hymns and singing games.
Sound effects—either commercially recorded or home-made.
Stories from children's literature, serials and anecdotes.
Tape recordings from school, home and on location.
Television programmes and video recordings.
Theme for a week or series of assemblies by school, class or individual presenters.
Visits—planning or reporting on a special visit.
Visitors—invite people to speak or be interviewed.

Resource Books—A Select Bibliography

1   Stories

Bad Boys ed. E. Colwell (Penguin/Puffin)
More Stories to Tell ed. E. Colwell (Penguin/Puffin)
My First Big Story Book ed. R. Bamberger (Penguin/Puffin)
My Second Big Story Book ed. R. Bamberger (Penguin/Puffin)
My Third Big Story Book ed. R. Bamberger (Penguin/Puffin)
Read Me a Story ed. F. Waters (Hamlyn/Bcaver)
Read Me Another Story ed. F. Waters (Hamlyn/Beaver)
Stories For Five Year Olds ed. S. & S. Corrin (Faber/Puffin)
Stories For Six Year Olds ed. S. & S. Corrin (Faber/Puffin)
Stories For Seven Year Olds ed. S. & S. Corrin (Faber/Puffin)
Tell Me a Story ed. E. Colwell (Penguin/Puffin)
Tell Me Another Story ed. E. Colwell (Penguin/Puffin)
Time for a Story ed. E. Colwell (Penguin/Puffin)

2   Poetry Books

Amazing Monsters ed. R. Fisher (Faber)
Bits and Pieces ed. P. Blakeley (Black)
The Book of a Thousand Poems ed. J. M. Macbain (Evans)
A Child's Garden of Verses R. L. Stevenson (Puffin)
Come Follow Me (Evans)
Fancy Free ed. D. Saunders and T. Williams (Evans)
A First Poetry Book ed. J. Foster (Oxford)
Full Swing ed. D. Saunders and V. Oliver (Evans)
Funny Rhymes ed. B. Ireson (Hamlyn/Beaver)
Happy Landings ed. H. Sergeant (Evans)
Junket and Jumbles ed. R. Wilson (Hamlyn/Beaver)
Junior Voices I ed. G. Summerfield (Penguin)
Meet My Folks Ted Hughes (Faber/Puffin)
Poems for Movement ed. E. J. M. Woodland (Evans)
The Puffin Book of Nursery Rhymes ed. I. and P. Opie (Penguin)
Rhyme Time ed. B. Ireson (Hamlyn/Beaver)
Round About Six ed. M. G. Rawlins (Warne)
Silly Verse for Kids S. Milligan (Dobson/Penguin)
Skipping Susan ed. E. J. M. Woodland (Evans)
The Swinging Rainbow ed. H. Sergeant (Evans)
Time's Delights ed. R. Wilson (Hamlyn/Beaver)
When a Goose Meets a Moose ed. C. Scott-Mitchell (Evans)
The Young Puffin Book of Verse ed. B. Ireson (Penguin)
Young Verse ed. J. Watson (Collins/Armada)

3 Song Books

Apusskidu B. Harrop (Black)
Come and Praise (BBC)
Faith, Folk and Clarity P. Smith (Galliard)
Harlequin D. Gadsby and B. Harrop (Black)
Morning Has Broken (Schofield and Sims)
New Child Songs (National Christian Education Council)
Okki-tokki-unga B. Harrop (Black)
Over and Over Again B. Ireson and C. Rowe (Hamlyn/Beaver)
The Oxford Nursery Song Book P. Buck (Oxford)
The Puffin Song Book L. Woodgate (Penguin)
Sing a Song 1 and 2 W. Bird and G. McAuliffe (Nelson)
Someone's Singing Lord (Black)
This Little Puffin E. Matterson (Puffin/Penguin)

4 Miscellanies of stories, poems and songs

Big Dipper J. Epstein, J. Factor, G. McKay and D. Rickards (OUP)
A Golden Land J. Reeves (Puffin/Penguin)
Seeing and Doing R. Farrimond and L. Sutch (Thames TV)
Sing, Say and Move J. McWilliam (Scripture Union)
Watch! T. Spanier (Macdonald/BBC)
Watch Again T. Spanier (Macdonald/BBC)

5 The School Assembly

First Assemblies R. Purton and C. Storey (Blackwell)
The Infant Teacher's Assembly Book D. M. Prescott (Blandford)
It's our Assembly A. Farncombe (NCEC)
Let's Start Where We Are M. M. Cantwell (DLT)
Our Turn for Assembly A. Farncombe (NCEC)
Themes and Prayers M. Ovens (Macmillan)
Together Today R. Fisher (Evans)

Note: *Together Today* also includes a list of music suitable for the school assembly, useful addresses and a calendar of festivals and anniversaries.

C. Uht

2